HARVEST OF HOPE

MY JOURNEY FROM FARM BOY

TO SUCCESSFUL DOCTOR

Dr. Charles Bingham

Daniel Gomez Enterprises L.L.C

Harvest of Hope:
By Dr. Charles Bingham
Published by Daniel Gomez Enterprises LLC / October 2025
Contact Info: (210) 663-5954 / Email: Info@DanielGomezGlobal.com
Copyright © 2025, Dr. Charles Bingham.

Dedication

This book is dedicated to God, my family, and friends. Without them, I would not be the man I am today. This book is just as much their accomplishment as it is mine. I was so fortunate to have the people who helped me get to where I am today. Some people had much bigger influences than others. However, they were all important. Thank you, and God Bless.

Table of Contents

Introduction

It is a great August day here in TN. I am looking out at the beautiful Smoky Mountains. I have had many challenges and obstacles throughout my life. Now things seem to be sailing better than before. I can now slow down and enjoy little moments like my children playing in the yard, drinking morning coffee, and watching wispy fog rise on the mountains. This book is to help you understand how I got here. It is to show you the steps I had to take, the things I had to learn to appreciate, and what I needed to get to this point in my life.

I started as a farm kid in Bray, Oklahoma. I thoroughly enjoyed my life on the farm growing up. I enjoyed the physical aspects of farming, mostly hauling square hay bales. It was great fun for me during the summer, because many people would not do it, so it was a fantastic way to earn some money, and I gained physical strength from it. Sometimes it seemed like I wanted to punish myself, but I always felt better after hauling hay; the work brings a clarity you'll rarely find elsewhere in life. I used the physicality of hay hauling as a challenge to get ready for fall sports. But there is a mental angle to it as well. They say if you look too far ahead, you'll give up because it seems like the field never ends, and the task is too big. The trick is to focus on the task at hand, the next bale in front of you, and when you conquer it, you do it again. This gave me a head start on practicing the mental toughness I knew I would need throughout my life. It helped me with the challenges I would face in life, all the way through medical school, my first few years as an attending physician, and later in business.

This book is my life story, telling how I went from a farm kid to a successful doctor. I invite you to sit back and enjoy reading about my life and the lessons I have learned along the way.

Chapter 1

We Made It

I feel complete sitting here watching Dr. Oakley, a Yukon Vet, with my children and wife. I have my purpose. I have my drive. I know what I stand for and who I am. I know that my children will not be cursed with the generational curses that have plagued my family in the past. We will be successful in setting our family on the correct path.

As a father, sometimes I get caught up in the day-to-day stuff and future plans, and I forget to enjoy the little moments. I am glad I have dedicated at least two hours a night to my children and family. I get snuggles on the couch. I get to watch my children's minds develop through play. I get to see their curiosity grow. Children are very fascinating. After watching Dr. Oakley, I see my daughter try to do the procedures on her stuffed animals. I have seen a wide range of surgery procedures from eye removals to castrations and even a few hernia repairs on her stuffed animals.

My son will assist with the anesthesia from time to time. My son is a typical young boy who is very punchy. He loves to play fight. He will occasionally have a softer side and want snuggles.

I have made it a priority to be present and focus on my family's life. When we're not watching Dr. Oakley or another educational film. My children like to play by wrestling. We can play wrestling for hours on end. My wife sometimes gets aggravated when I throw the children across the room onto the couch. However, they giggle, bounce up, and come back for more. My son has no fear. He also has a very protective streak. If I even pretend to go after his mom or his sister, he will immediately take me out at the knees. Then he and his sister will climb on top of me and try to hold me down. They will say, "pinned you again, daddy". Sometimes they like to pretend that I am Jörmungandr, the Midgard Serpent, my son is Thor, and my daughter is Freya. We must keep tradition, and Thor will kill me with his trusty hammer, Mjolnir. My children's imaginations are amazing. I want to encourage them more and more to keep using their imagination. This is why I have to be present. I have been many villains during these wrestling matches, from Scar from The Lion King, Gaston from Beauty and the Beast, Hades from Hercules, and occasionally Green Goblin from Spider-Man and friends. These are beautiful moments that must never be missed.

I have made it a point to bring a sense of calm to my family. We will dive deeper into this later in this book. My education and life experiences taught me that children need a calm place.

Children's lives are chaotic enough. It's up to the parents to provide structure and support in the house. My wife and I run the house; the children do not. This, in and of itself, gives children a sense of calmness. I will be my children's rock. I will be their constant state of serenity in this erratic world.

Some people let external factors dictate their actions, such as a boss, acquaintances, or perceived social norms. Sometimes you must find yourself before you can make it in this world. We have to stop listening to external factors/opinions about our life. For the longest time, I let other people tell me what was important. I even listened to them from time to time. Now I know what is important. I learned to prioritize my family's needs and goals over those of others. Everyone needs to figure out what is important to them. Don't just listen to other people. I highly suggest you take some time with yourself and figure out what makes you tick. You should take some time to sit in silence with yourself to find out what is important to you. You will be surprised by what your true calling is. Stay true to yourself and you will have a better chance of success. This change in me got me to the point of making a huge career change. I gave up the secure corporate physician job that paid very well to chase a dream that kept coming to me over the last decade. It has been a success. I stayed true to the destiny that was put in my head repeatedly.

I cannot take credit for everything. My wife has been instrumental in everything that I've done. She's always been supportive of my dreams. I have been supportive of her dreams as well. We are a great team. We play off each other's strengths. She never tells me I can't do anything. She tells me, "You will find a way". She knows my tenacity and my no-quit attitude. She will offer words of support when needed and, without hesitation, light a fire under my butt when I am procrastinating. My wife is a very successful family medicine physician as well. She is very much the classic book nerd who has had the goal of being a doctor from birth. She and I are both very passionate about patients. We are both driven to give them the best possible care as physicians.

I have overcome many obstacles in my life that have led me to my position. I love how the obstacles in our lives make us who we are. These obstacles are character-building events. Anyone who is going to be successful has to deal with obstacles. These obstacles will be discussed throughout this book. These obstacles have led me to be confident in who I am. I am a loving father. I am a caring husband. I am the protector of my family. I am the one who shoulders the responsibility for creating generational wealth for my family. I am a successful doctor who cares deeply about his patients. I am the friend that people call on when they are in need.

One of the best things about putting yourself into uncomfortable situations is the gains you can make. One of the best gains is relationships with people. People are the reason anyone is here. People are essential for everybody and their success. This is not a book about how I made it to the pinnacle of my life without anyone's help. This book is more about the hidden angels that have helped me through my times of need. Anyone who thinks they made it through life without help is a spectacular fool. There's always been someone there helping you in some way.

Yes, someone can have all the drive in the world, and that's what people see. They see a person who is driven and willing to do the necessary work to succeed. Therefore, they are eager to help them. This is how I got relationships with the right people at the right time. I have a network of friends. This network will not be as big as most people's. My network of friends is the equivalent of Wyatt Earp and Doc Holiday in *Tombstone*. If you have not seen this film, congratulations, you have homework, go and watch it!! After doing so, you'll understand the true meaning of "friends". I have made it because I have friends in my life who are actual friends. They are not the typical fake-ass people who will run away when hard times await me. They are friends who help in any way they can when times are hard. Sometimes all that is needed is a different perspective.

I invite you to come on this journey down memory lane. You will find things in this book to motivate you. You will find some things very amusing. You will learn from my path. So, buckle up and enjoy the ride.

Life Lessons

1. Know who you are!!
2. Know what you want in Life and why.
3. Get people who have similar goals to help push you.

Questions for the Reader

1. Do you schedule time to remember who you are in life?

_____

_____

2. Do you make time to question what you want in life?

_____

_____

3. What's a main takeaway from this chapter?

_____

_____

Chapter 2

Life on the Farm

It was a fall day in 1995. I was feeding cows with my brother and mother when we noticed one cow was missing. We went to look for her. It was unlike this cow to go missing. When you have lived on a small farm, you know each animal individually and their personality. This cow never skipped a meal. In fact, she was the cow that was always in the way so that you couldn't spread out the cattle cubes to the rest of the cows. She wanted the pile in front of her to keep it for herself. So, we set off driving through the pasture looking for her. We found her at the top of the hill, lying on her side, and her stomach was extremely bloated. It was the first time I had seen a cow this way. The three of us tried to put her back on her feet. We didn't know what we were doing at that time. We had just gotten cattle two years prior. I had not seen a situation like this yet. So, after several failed attempts, we went down the road to get someone with more experience. My grandpa had worked with animals his whole life on many different farms. He had the knowledge that we desperately needed at that time.

When we got to grandpa's house and told him about the situation, he just laughed at us for trying to push the cow up on her feet. He slowly got up from the kitchen table, put on his boots, and a light jacket. I remember him saying, "Come on, let's fix her." Instead of heading to the truck like I figured. He headed to the shed. He pulled out a garden hose. He tuned to me and asked me if I wanted to cut her side or use the hose. He said either way would work, but I had to choose. At that time, I didn't like cutting things and didn't want to hurt the cow. So, of course, we chose the hose. He smiled and laughed, saying, "The hose will be more difficult and take longer". Then we headed out back to the pasture. Once we got on the hill where the cow was, he told Mom and my brother to hold the cow's head down. He took the hose and shoved it into her mouth and down to her stomach.

As an 8-year-old child, I was interested in this, so I watched it intently. The next thing I remember is a gush of air from the hose, my brother and mom started gagging and saying something stunk to high hell. A few seconds later, the bloated gas from the cow reached my nose, a smell you'll never forget. My stomach turned at that nice aroma of partially digested fermented grass. I wanted to vomit. However, my grandfather told me to go push on the stomach to help get all the air out. As I pushed on the stomach of this cow, I could feel the pressure reducing in her stomach. It was fascinating that we were fixing her without the help of a vet. I asked Grandpa if we should call the vet. He looked up and asked, "Why do we need a bill from them? She will be fixed in a few minutes". He was laughing the whole time at my mom, my brother, and I. The smell didn't seem to bother him. Everyone else in our group had difficulty keeping down their breakfasts.

After getting the pressure off the cow's stomach, my grandpa said it was time to get her feet under her. So, my mom, brother, and I got on one side of the cow and pushed her onto her feet. Once her feet were underneath her, she got up easily. My grandfather just looked at us while sitting on his 5-gallon bucket. He said we needed to watch her walk around for a while. Most likely, she would be fine. I needed to check on her a couple of times a day. Now we needed to fence off the area with the clover growing. He said that was what caused her to get bloated.

This experience in my life has taught me that sometimes you don't need so-called professionals. You need people with expertise to help guide you in life. My grandfather had a ton of experience in multiple aspects of life. He is one of the smartest men I have ever known. He actually did not complete high school. I believe it was the sixth grade that he completed. After that, he had to stop school to help raise and pay for his brothers' and sisters' food and clothes. He was the oldest, so it was his responsibility to help provide money for his family. He started working multiple jobs. Having a grandpa like this taught me never to look down on anyone. You can always learn from anybody, no matter who or what their qualifications are. Never to look at someone's credentials and think that is all that matters. I have been around many highly qualified professionals who can't make good decisions if it hits them in the face. Then there are people like my grandpa who can solve complex equations in his head faster than I could on a calculator. He had great advice on many other things in life as well. He was one of my first and most powerful mentors in life. He was a man with humble beginnings who lived life to the best of his ability. He seemed happy most of the time, if not all the time. I enjoyed the lessons he taught me.

Life for a boy in small-town Oklahoma is pretty awesome. I could run around in the woods and blow off steam. I could get into a situation where I would have to think to get myself out of. I was fortunate to be free to go into the woods behind my house and walk for hours. It's very peaceful, and you can go through things and learn more about yourself mentally.

This ability to get away came in very handy throughout my life. I was able to disconnect from reality. I was able to find myself. I realized that if anything was going to happen in my life, it was up to me and no one else. Throughout life, you're going to have people who will help you. Ultimately, it's up to you to take the help and make the most of it. Only you and God know your plan. Hell, I didn't even know my plan. Therefore, I had to rely on God. This red dirt in Oklahoma allowed me to be grounded and keep moving forward.

This became very important in the summer of 1998. I was playing summer baseball, and we were on a trip to Oklahoma City for a baseball tournament. I had been feeling fatigued and run-down for about a week. My mom and dad had a feeling that something was possibly wrong. However, they couldn't put their finger on it. The whole ride up to Oklahoma City, we had to stop every 15-30 minutes so I could pee. Once we got to Oklahoma City, we checked into the Holiday Inn Hotel. I went swimming like all the other kids; however, I didn't swim long because I was tired. I lay down for bed, and I kept getting up every 15 to 30 minutes peeing all night. The next morning, we went to breakfast at McDonald's. Whenever we were out, I had to have my sausage biscuit, my favorite breakfast meal. I typically would eat two. However, today I took one bite and was nauseous. My nose was on fire; it felt like I was breathing in acid. We went back to the hotel. I was getting ready to change into my swim shorts to swim again. My parents saw the way my body looked at that time. I looked like a skeleton of my former self. I was dehydrated and would later find out my body was eating itself, breaking down fat and muscle, trying to stay alive. My parents immediately checked us out of the hotel and loaded the family in the car, including my dad, mom, brother, sister, and me. We started the drive to our medical clinic, which was an hour away. There was minimal talking the entire trip to Lawton, OK. The only one complaining was my sister because she did not get to stay at the hotel and swim in the pool. She was 4 years old then, so that is fair; she was disappointed.

Once we got to the clinic, a doctor ordered a blood sugar check. My blood sugar read high but was not readable on their monitor. He then turned to my parents and told them to take me to the Emergency Room down the road. He advised my parents that I was diabetic. I had no clue what that meant. I was an 11-year-old boy who was supposed to play in a baseball tournament that day. I could tell it was serious when my mom started crying immediately. My dad stayed stoic. He grabbed my shoulder and said, "Yes, we'll go right now".

The next thing I knew, I was in the emergency room with nurses trying to put IVs in my arm. They had a hard time getting an IV on me since I was so dehydrated. I think three different nurses tried twice each. Finally, the last one got the IV. The nurse was able to draw my blood and then brought in numerous IV bags. I knew they were trying to help, so I didn't move while they were doing all the things I needed to have done. I don't remember the physician's name; I do remember what he looked like. He was a young physician, maybe in his upper 30s or low 40s. He came in and talked to my parents. I overheard some conversations about the fact that there was no cure. It would be something I would live with for the rest of my life. My mom started crying again. I could even see the worry in my father's eyes. It was at that time that I thought I was dying. I was so sleepy from the nights of not sleeping because I was constantly urinating, hungry from my body starving from not being able to process glucose for energy, and now scared of dying. I soon passed out from exhaustion.

When I woke, my dad told me I had been asleep for over two days. My body needed rest, lots of fluids, and IV medication. I was still in the ICU. At the same time, a short Filipino doctor came in. My first impression of her was that she was very intense. My dad acknowledged her as if he had spoken to her multiple times. However, I was conscious for the first time since being in the ER. She looked at me and said that I had been a very sick boy. My blood sugar had gone up to 876. She informed me that I had gone into what is known as DKA (diabetic ketoacidosis). My body did not produce insulin anymore and could not use the glucose in my blood. Therefore, my body started eating itself, producing ketones. This made my body acidic. I then understood why I had lost so much weight and why I had the acid smell in my nose. It was almost like acetone. The last piece of the puzzle was why I was urinating so much. She explained that this was because my body was trying to eliminate all the sugar in my bloodstream. So, the kidneys were dumping as much sugar into my urine as possible, which made me pee every 15-30 minutes.

She then proceeded to tell me I would need a medication called insulin for the rest of my life. I asked if that was a pill. She proceeded to tell me no, that I would have to get used to giving myself shots multiple times a day. My dad said that he could give me the shot if needed. She looked at me and then my father and said, "No, he has to live with this. He will have to learn to give himself shots". Being a farm kid, I was picturing an 18-gauge cow needle going into my side or arm or something like that. She then brought in an orange and a diabetic needle that I had to use to give my orange a shot. I remember looking at the needle and thinking that it was tiny. I laughed. My father looked at me, and I said, "This is going to be nothing". How naïve I was.

When I was first diagnosed with diabetes at the age of 11, I learned within the first week after being discharged that my life would forever be different. I would not have been able to be what I wanted to be since I was a young child. I wanted to become a Navy SEAL. I would watch the training videos of the Navy Seals going through hell week. I would also daydream about fighting or gathering intel in a faraway land. I would be the best version of myself day in and day out. This was gone as soon as I talked to a Navy recruiter. Yes, you read that right, I was talking to recruiters at the age of 11. I was a different type of kid.

In sports, I soon realized that I would have a much harder time getting play time in any sport. My baseball coach did not want to play me anymore. I cannot blame him. He did not know what having diabetes meant for a kid playing a sport. I grew up in a small rural community in Oklahoma. As far as I knew, I was the only person with type 1 diabetes. The town population was 1200ish around that time. Anything different there might as well have been from a different world. I played on the bench until I proved to my coaches that I wouldn't fall over dead while playing. I did have to put extra effort into playing sports. I had to calculate the time spent playing and the number of insulin shots I needed to be safe. Too much insulin, I could pass out from hypoglycemia (low blood sugar), and not enough insulin, my reaction time would be slow, and I would be useless to the team. These were just extra challenges that I had to deal with in order to participate in sports.

But what hurt the worst after being diagnosed with diabetes was being treated differently by family. Family is supposed to be a safe place. However, this was not true for me. My mother was dwelling in her self-pity and always making everything about her. She would put on a good face in front of other people. However, I knew from a young age that if I was going to be well, it was entirely up to me to take care of myself and my diabetes. Therefore, I learned how to take care of myself. I gave myself shots and pricked my finger to test my blood sugar multiple times a day.

This is when living in the small rural town of Bray, OK, was a good thing. I was able to take time for myself and refocus. I was able to spend time in nature. I don't think there was a pond or a creek within a 5-mile radius of my house that I did not know of. I would either walk to them by myself or have friends who would go with me—a lot of times, we would catch dinner and bring it home. I learned how to fillet a fish by age six or seven. I was able to cook at the same age. Playing outside with my neighbors, I forged friendships that would last a lifetime. It wasn't until I was 12 that I had a four-wheeler to drive me to places. I bought the damn thing by myself. I had saved up enough money from my chickens to pay cash. This made my life getting to and from the ponds and creeks carrying the fish bag much easier.

Yes, I raised chickens, pigs, hunting dogs, horses, an occasional goat, and cattle. However, the chickens were all mine. It was up to me to buy the feed. My dad helped me by taking me to the feed store. He instilled a sense of responsibility by making them mine. Anything that would happen to them, good or bad, was my fault. This is one of the good things about being raised on a farm: the sense of responsibility you gain for others relying on you for their survival. If you don't care for your animals, they die, and you go hungry. I enjoyed life on the farm. Animals are far more real than most people could ever be to you. You know within an instant if a rooster will chase you, try to flog you, or mind their own business and eat their food. You can read most animals' body language to see whether or not they're mad or hurt. Animals want space, love, food, and water. It was very peaceful raising animals.

With farming, you always had something that needed to be done. It instilled a sense of accomplishment after achieving my goals for the day. Some of the most challenging days of my life came from farming. Whether it was building a fence or hauling hay. I'm not talking about hauling hay that is in round bales, where you just push the damn button. I'm talking about square bales; throwing them onto the trailer, hauling them, and unloading them into a barn. This is nothing but brute force. You are moving these objects with your own hands. I wish I were still in the shape I was in my younger years when I was hauling hay during the summer for extra cash.

Hay hauling was one of my 1st jobs. I vividly remember the summer I was 15 years old, working with my friend as I threw the last bale of hay into the barn. I looked at my best friend, Tyler. He was just as dirty and tired as I was. We just completed another full day of hauling hay. This was the fourth day in a row. Our hands were cut up and worn from the wire that holds the hay bales together. We had just completed slightly over 12,000 bales of hay in four days. Looking back now, that's a lot of damn hay. We never quit. We accomplished the goal and moved on to the next challenge. I started hauling hay for my father when I was probably 8 years old. Hauling hay is not a glamorous job. It is a necessary job. It is a character-building job. You put on your gloves. You look across the field at this impossible task. Hay hauling taught me not to look at the whole picture continuously. You would never start if you looked across the field and saw every hay bale there. You look at the section of hay in front of you and realize that's not so hard. Doing this allows you to take bite-sized chunks out of a considerable task, and before long, the task is complete. You do not get overwhelmed; you do what is necessary and get the job done. You pick up one hay bale at a time, throw it into the truck or trailer. You keep moving down the line. While doing this, your body becomes accustomed to the sting in your hands from the wire, and the ache in your legs, and back after you've been at it for a long time. For life on the farm, we know we have to put so many hay bales back during the spring and summer so that the cows can survive the winter, as the grass in Oklahoma goes dormant during the Winter. Without hay, your investment and livelihood can be lost in one season. The work of hauling hay is an investment to ward off starvation in your cows during the winter.

Growing up in a small town helped me develop several tools I would need as an adult. The first being resilient or tenacious. I knew after my diagnosis of diabetes that I would have to work harder than most kids to get playing time. My father helped me with this. Shortly after my diagnosis, I realized I wasn't getting to play like I used to. I didn't understand why, because I still played the same, actually a little better now that I don't feel like crap all the time. My father told me life was unfair, that just because I came back and could still play the way I used to, didn't mean I got my position back. He advised me that from now on, I'd probably have to work harder to get the same amount of playing time. Not to get my head down and be a victim, but to accept the responsibility of playing time was mine, nobody else's. This helped set me up for developing responsibility over my life instead of blaming others. I accepted the responsibility and placed that onto my shoulders, not anyone else's.

Next, I learned the importance of delayed gratification. Sometimes things have to build or grow over time. I knew this, watching animals grow. This is more evident with the chickens than anything else. Maybe it was because their time from hatching to being able to sell is much quicker than that of cows. Also, I was able to sell eggs as well as chickens. I did not get rich quickly with this scenario. However, I did have quite a bit of money as a young child, enough to buy a four-wheeler by myself. I was also the sibling who always had money in their account. I saw the value of hard work by caring for the animals and ensuring they had what they needed. Hauling hay is still one of the hardest jobs I've ever had. You can learn a lot about yourself in a hayfield. I think this should be a rite of passage for some children. I know some people will read this statement and think that's barbaric. I don't care.

Lastly, growing up in a small town allowed me to get out of the house and judge whether or not a situation was safe for me. I do feel bad for children today. They can't even cross the street without parents freaking out. Hell, I saw two days ago on the news where a parent was getting arrested because their 10-year-old child was walking a block down the road. This is completely asinine and absurd. Children need to be able to figure things out on their own sometimes. They need the ability to engage in dangerous situations with some supervision. Children need to play together and learn social dynamics from playing with other children. They need to be able to figure out conflict resolution amongst themselves.

I had the ability to grow up. It just makes me sad that my children may not have this chance. Hell, look at the playground nowadays, there's not a merry-go-round in sight. Everything is cushioned and padded; there are no scraped knees, bruised elbows, or God forbid, a child in a cast. When's the last time you saw a child with a cast? Not that I want children to get hurt, I want them to realize there are consequences for their actions. Because if they go through life without ever suffering any consequences, you get young adults who do the most outrageous things, and then it hurts them or someone else severely. It's like the implications of their action had no bearing on their mind. Just because we can prevent almost all childhood injuries does not necessarily mean we should. Sometimes kids need to fool around and find out.

I was able to leave the house pretty much when I wanted to. My father would ask, "Where are you planning on going?". I was free to leave if I could answer that question. Half the time, I didn't even ask. I just got up and walked out. Because most of the time, he knew exactly where I was going. Most of the time, I was going to listen to the hounds chase a coon up a tree. I would unleash the dogs and hunt in the pastures behind my house all night. I grew up raccoon hunting. There was a big creek that ran behind my childhood home. The first time I went raccoon hunting by myself behind the house, I was 14 or 15 years old. I had two dogs, a headlight, and a Bowie knife. I did not carry a gun with me because it was not season at that time for coons. Most kids today are scared to walk to a vehicle in the dark, parked right in front of their house.

Growing up on a farm in a small town, I believe, is one of the best things that has happened to me. I was able to see what true freedom was. I was not confined to one small space. I had the entire pasture behind my house to play, and everybody knew everyone. I could run and play at friends' houses without my parents taking me. I was able to achieve what some psychologists/psychiatrists call playful learning. It saddens me that I may be one of the last generations to be immersed in this playful learning. In today's world, parents are too fearful to let their children play. Parents will not let their children out of their sight. My parents trusted the adults in the community to help watch out for us. If I was doing something wrong, it would get back to my parents rather quickly. I also remember being disciplined by my friends' parents and other adults in the community. I was never abused by any of the other adults in my community. Sometimes what is needed as a growing male child is a correction factor, either a swat on the back of the head or a disciplinary swat on the butt. Some people reading this are going to say that this is child abuse. However, it is what most male children need occasionally.

I will never forget my time in Bray, Oklahoma, and have cherished memories. I still have my friends there that I can call on. If you ever want to get grounded back in reality. I encourage you to go back to your hometown for a visit. You will get made fun of like you did as a kid, which can be greatly humbling. It does not matter where you made it to in life. You will get targeted just like you are back at the old hangout place from high school. They will remind you of things you forgot and reminisce about who you were back then. It is good to see how everyone has grown and changed since our childhood.

The people from my community were pretty awesome. Being from a small town, I could not get by with much without my family hearing about it. Most of the time, the news would reach home before I did. It is funny to think back at my dad just waiting for me to come home one night after he heard that my friends and I had a bonfire in the woods. He just wanted to know I was okay, then he went to bed. There was no scolding or late-night talking to. It was just verifying that I was still breathing and did not drive home drunk. It was one of the ways my dad showed that he trusted me to make the correct choices in life.

Growing up, bonfires would happen a few times a year. Yes, we did have alcohol at these events. There were occasional fights at these events as well. This was the boys just blowing off steam. Most of the time, we would be friends again after the fight. Everyone had weapons, from knives to guns, either on us or in the trucks. No one ever thought of using them. It was some of the best fun of my life, sitting under the night sky by a fire, laughing at each other, and doing goofy things. My goal was to have fun and be myself. We had our share of rich kids, middle-class, and poor kids. Out here, we were all the same. If someone stepped too far out of line, it was corrected instantly, and the fun would continue.

The adults in the community had high expectations of the children and held each accountable. If you messed up, any of the adults would correct you. I remember occasionally getting in trouble by either Tyler's dad or Trey's dad. They never beat us. In a small town, most of the men are rugged and work physical jobs. You'd better stay on their good sides, and when they correct you, you'd better damn well listen to them. Some of these men work on the oil rigs before all the new machines that made it a safer field. These men would constantly work with chains and heavy pipes. Some of their grip strength was off the charts. If you didn't listen, you would learn the hard way. I was a fast learner. Most of my friends were growing up.

The woman in the community also knew how to get the best out of most of the children. They are some of the sweetest women in the world. But don't get on their bad side. They will cuss you like a sailor. If I had it to do over again, I would pester them a little more, just for the amusement. These women would think it was a sin if you left their house hungry. My grandmother and aunts took this to heart. You would get a meal if you even looked at food in their house. I miss these women terribly.

I could keep going on and on about the life of my small town. There were so many great aspects of it. The men, the women, and the school all helped shape who I am today. I had so many teachers from Bray, Oklahoma to help me along the way. Even though I do not live in Oklahoma anymore, I still know that this is my hometown. Whenever I get the chance to go back, I like seeing the people I grew up with. It is crazy how to this day, just going to pick up groceries with my dad, I can run into a number of people from my childhood. We can just talk like we are back 20 years ago. Who knows, maybe one day I'll move back.

I wish some things could go back in time. Our children would benefit greatly from a town like the one I grew up in. Men and women set standards, men hold everyone to them, and women provide the needed nurturing support. Men are the masculine models and protectors of the community and way of life.

Life Lessons

1.   Never interrupt children playing. Let them figure things out.

2.   Remember, credentials do not mean everything. Listen to and learn from everyone.

3.   Never doubt the importance of your old friends and our hometown community.

4.   Allow children to take risks.

5.   Know the value of your challenges growing up and what they taught you.

Questions for the Reader

1.   What is something you had to overcome that improved your life?

_____

_____

2.   What are some crazy things you did as a child that bring back good memories today?

_____

_____

3.   What is something you overcame that seemed impossible at first?

_____

_____

4. Where do you go to get away from things and clear your head?

_____

_____

5. What is our main takeaway from this chapter?

_____

_____

Chapter 3

Broken Home

Life in small-town Oklahoma was great. I could do many things today's kids could only dream of doing. However, in life, everything good can also come with bad things. Being in a small town meant little entertainment for kids or adults. Some of the adults in my village were either addicted to alcohol, drugs, or both. I can honestly say my father never really drank, and he damn sure never did drugs. I can only remember him having one or two beers at a time. On the other hand, my mother loved being the life of the party. From a young age, it was apparent that if she were not the center of attention, there would be hell to pay. My father normally paid the price. She would think someone was getting more attention than her and start throwing a fit. I remember her screaming at my father, throwing things at him, and hitting him. She had no shame or sense of dignity when she got in these moods. She caused scenes in front of family and friends alike.

This wrath occasionally found me or my siblings. She would yell and belittle us. She would also, on occasion, cross the line into physical abuse. She would hit us with whatever was in her hands in those moments. One night, she hit me in the face with a curtain rod, leaving a gash on the side of my face. Fortunately, we were well-versed in skin repairs from farming, and the resulting scar is small. The worst time was when she went after my brother with a marble pie-rolling pin. I tried to intervene and help my brother, but I got caught on the side of the head instead. That one left a concussion. Of course, we did not get checked out; I had had concussions before from wrestling and football, and a doctor's visit was an expense and a paper trail. Mom just said, "Don't tell your father". I was 14 at the time.

Physical abuse was the least of our problems, though. My mother was one of the best at emotional manipulation and inflicting psychological damage. She was this way because of the way she was raised. She had many traumas in her childhood and hadn't learned to deal with them. Of course, I did not understand that in my childhood, when she was forever playing the victim and making everyone else feel bad for the problems in her life. She was the most righteous in her mind, and others were evil or out to get her. She used her children as her ever-present therapists to help with any problem. She would rely on us to faithfully listen to her personal problems, ranging from disagreements with other parents to issues with her and my father. As a byproduct, we would get blamed if things didn't go her way.

She always wanted to be the "cool mom". That meant she wanted to be the one throwing the parties and creating the good times. For her, any attention was her drug of choice. Speaking of drugs, she indulged in them as well. She smoked weed with anyone. Her preferred actual drugs were pills, both opioids and benzodiazepines (Xanax). She stayed high most of the time after her sister died. I remember catching her one day with one of my classmates' brothers. They were smoking meth. She still played the victim, claiming it was not bad. I realized even before the meth that

I couldn't rely on my mother for most things. She was an addict and would not be the person I would call for help.

Once all these behaviors got old, my older brother and I found ways to distance ourselves from her, and we did. Regretfully, this put more of my mom's focus on my little sister. Sometimes, especially when you're young, you do not see all the second and third-order effects your actions will have. My sister was much younger than my brother and me. She didn't learn as fast as we did. We tried to help her, but she did not listen or want our help. My mother did a psychological number on her from early childhood. Mom would refer to my sister as "the child only my dad wanted". She thought it was just a funny joke, but after being told that for so long, my sister believed it. My sister started seeking validation from our mom when she was very young. My mom leaned into my sister and her friends' lives growing up, and my sister got caught up in Mom's drama for over two decades. My mom surprised even me when I later found out she was supplying my sister opioids to stay relevant in her life. My sister became an addict at 14 years old because of my mother.

The way my mother was able to infiltrate my sister's life messed up her normal development. The psychological games that my mother played also seem to affect her more visibly than my brother and I. My sister always seems to run back to my mother. She could not break from the need that my mother had for her. I am unsure if it was just my sister's addiction that was dependent on my mother for so long, or if she felt bad for my mother. These demons continue to plague my sister well into her adulthood. This has caused my sister to lose her family as an adult and her independence for almost 2 decades of her life. It was the start she had that paved this path for her. I do regret leaving my sister in my mother's drama and drugs.

However, my sister made it very clear she wanted nothing to do with me as a teenager. She was a typical teenager in rebellion against the person who had raised her. My mother knew exactly how to manipulate that situation-she named me "the golden child" to play off my sister's insecurities and feelings of inadequacy compared to my apparent success at school and home. She continually drove a wedge between my sister and me. My sister resented me since I was trying to pull her away from the situation. I was my sister's villain. In her mind, she wanted to do the opposite of anything I advised her to do. I remember my sister telling me, "I am glad you are leaving. You are the worst brother. I can finally live life without you," when I told her I was leaving to live in an apartment a town over. I will not lie that destroyed me on the inside. She was like a daughter to me more than a sister. I knew that anything I said would not help. She was following in my mother's footsteps.

The behavior that hurt the most from my mother was the constant embarrassment at social events growing up. She showed up under the influence of pills to these events, slurring her words and not making sense most of the time. People seemed shocked when talking to her; they often had to ask her to clarify what she was saying. She was very difficult to follow in conversation when she was under the influence.

Mom also brought people who were not safe for her children to be around into the house. In a small town there is a very clear delineation of who is considered "accepted" and who is a "social outcast". My mom gravitated to these few outcasts our area and brought in other similar outsiders to fill her world. She always wanted to "rescue" everyone but she never could set boundaries. My parents lived in different socials worlds, as their child I straddled both. In my dad's world I went hunting and fishing and played sports. As a child, I had pills offered to me. I had alcohol offered to me numerous times. I even had other "hard-core" drugs offered to me on multiple occasions from my mother's so-called friends. They would say it is okay to try; you will not get addicted to just trying these. I remember watching people snort pills off the kitchen cabinet. They would put the straw in my hand and say, "Give it a try". I would say no, and then be informed that I was a square and no fun by the older teenagers and adults my mother brought into the house. I am not sure what kept making me say no all those years. I was tempted; however, some voice in my head kept saying, "DO NOT BE LIKE THEM." Therefore, I kept refusing to do any drugs. I have never done any form of illegal drugs.

I don't want this to sound like a hate session on my mother. My mother did have some good qualities. I believe she did love us in her own way. I hope she can overcome her demons and find peace in her mind. I want to give examples of things that I had to overcome, things that I think many people can relate to. Her mental disorders made her an unfit parent. She could not put anyone else's needs above her own. This led to all her children having some issues that needed to be resolved. Some of us are still working on things. To this day, I am working on breaking generational curses. My mother was the way she was because of her upbringing. She was neglected as a child and manipulated by the adults in her life. Her father left at a young age. She suffered through several severe forms of abuse. If she chooses to write a book, she can disclose them; that is her story to tell. As an adult, she has a dependent/histrionic personality disorder, compounding her childhood events that likely led to her addictions, which, in turn, made everything worse. My point is not to go into detail or cast irreparable shame. This is for you, the reader, to realize that it's not where you start that matters. It's about how much you want out of your current situation. How hard are you willing to work to get out of that damn spot? Be a little better each day, and you will succeed before you know it.

I have put in many hours of work with coaches, meditating, and self-reflecting to keep myself from placing these same generational curses on my children. This is not something you snap out of overnight. You'll have to dig deep to determine what you want your children and family to get from you. You have to decide to take the gut check and fix yourself. No matter what you do, you will always have that little child inside you. The little insecure child inside of you is the one who grew up with you through those adverse events and is still scared of all the things you forgot about. It is hard not to revert to that child in stressful times. However, overcoming these traumas in life with hard internal work is possible.

I learned the hard way that suppression can only work for so long. I tried bottling things up for many years, well into my early 20s. I started consuming alcohol regularly. One morning after an all-night party, I had a psychology midterm test. I knew I had to get to the school to take the test even though I still felt the effects of the absinthe from the night before. A friend of mine had brought this back from overseas on his R&R. It had the actual hallucinogen in it, and we decided we were going to hallucinate. For some reason, drinking alcohol to hallucinate was okay in my mind, even if drugs weren't. For the record, Absinthe is still one of the nastiest drinks I've ever tasted. I drank my bottle plus half of another bottle. I was great at consuming hard liquor at that time. Looking back, I was trying to numb something. I stopped drinking around three in the morning and got up at seven to drive 40 minutes to the school to take the test. I was disappointed I did not hallucinate the night before. Barely staying awake on the road, heard a big-ass dog barking next to me in the truck. I ended up running off the road and into a ditch. I was looking in the cab of the car for the dog, it was not there. Hell, I seriously thought a hell-hound was after me. I sat there for a few moments, realizing it had to be the hallucinogen from the absinthe finally kicking in. Luckily, my beat-up farm truck didn't take any damage going into the ditch, and I finally made it to the university. Before taking my test, one of the girls sitting next to me in class asked if I was okay because it was one of the first times I showed up visibly impaired to class. I told her I was fine, but she knew I wasn't. That damned hell-hound set up shop in the brick wall on the second floor of the psychology building and barked at me the whole way through the mid-term. After the test, I remember going to the bathroom and looking in the mirror. I was a freaking wreck. I looked like hell. I knew I smelled like hell from all the smoke and alcohol the night before. I knew that this was not the person I wanted to be. So, I decided then and there that something had to change. Since that day, I have not been that drunk again. I may have one or two beers, but I stay away from hard liquor now. On a funny note, that is the highest grade I have ever achieved on a Psychology test. You need to be a little off to do well in Psychology.

One thing I have learned through all of this is that someone is watching over me. I had several times when someone would come out of nowhere and help in one way or another. These people may have only been present for a while or may have been a big part of my life, but these hidden angels have always been a blessing. Probably the biggest angel in my life was my grandmother. From a young age, I started to lean on my grandma for the nurturing support a child needs. She did a fantastic job with all her grandchildren. She taught me how to cook. She helped calm me down when I was in need of a calmer mind. She stood up for me and my siblings against my mother. She never shied away from taking care of us. We often sat at her kitchen table and listened to her and my grandpa chatting about life. I learned so much from them. I learned that my grandfather only went to school until the 6th grade. As the oldest, he had to quit school to help work and pay for his brothers' and sisters' food and clothes. He worked hard all his life. My grandparents' house was always a safe place to be in. You never left hungry. My grandma's cooking was so damn good.

She made everything with love. It did not matter if it was just a sandwich or her fried chicken (that was my favorite). It was all made with love. As a child, I felt love in everything she did for us. It was what I needed. My grandparents helped to teach us the old ways of life. I don't care what anyone says, the old ways are superior to this new life fad crap. I miss family values being important. I enjoyed watching my grandparents work through difficult conversations. They always worked on their problems instead of sweeping them under the rug. This showed me that anything worth having in life will require work and sacrifice.

My grandma was the positive, feminine role model I needed to grow up. She was always there for me until she passed away. I will remember the beautiful and challenging person she was. I miss the talks on the porch, the Yahtzee and Phase 10 games, and her encouraging smile. She was a one-of-a-kind lady.

Life is kind to no one, so don't think someone has never had to struggle in some way because their story looks different. Understand that a family can look normal and healthy from the outside, but inside the house, there is darkness. I have seen this many times over the years. I have learned that everyone's challenges are different. So be kind to others and yourself. Know that the child inside you who cried when nobody listened is still there. Dig deep and help that child. Life goes much better once you decide to get friends who can help you. I looked for help in the wrong places initially. When I finally decided that I needed to fix myself for my family, my life changed for the best version of me. I have friends who tell me when I am messing up. The friend who grabs you and tells you the truth is what you need in life. They will take you to bigger and better things. My grandmother was that person when I was young. Now I have two friends who will tell me exactly what they think, I may not always do what they feel is best, but I listen. They also listen to me. Be that friend, please, help each other out of darkness. The way out of darkness is by collaboration, mentorship, and work to achieve a goal.

Life Lessons

1. Always remember that you can accomplish great things regardless of your starting point.

2. You will have obstacles in life. It is up to you to overcome them.

3. Never doubt the importance of friends and community to help you overcome your difficulties.

Questions for the Reader

1. What are some obstacles that hold you back?

    _____

    _____

2. What are you still angry about that has happened to you in the past? What has holding on to that anger cost you?

    _____

    _____

3. Who is the person/people you go to for help? Can they challenge you to be better, or do they just tell you what you want to hear?

    _____

    _____

4. What is the main takeaway from this chapter?

    _____

    _____

Chapter 4

Anything is Possible

I will fight and overcome all obstacles because Christ strengthens me. I have always seemed to keep moving forward and rolling with the punches. As you recall, in school, I had a hard time getting any playing time at first because of my size and the fact that I had diabetes. Even with diabetes, I played baseball, football, and weight-lifted. From the first time playing football, I was a kid possessed. Again, I didn't see much playing time initially. I was the kid with a disease that scared people. I made up my mind to make them have to play me. I would be the littlest guy on the field, looking for the biggest guy to knock the shit out of. I would hold nothing back in practice or in games. I would act almost like a kamikaze. Once I found a target, it was time to destroy that target or myself. It was this reckless abandon that got me respect from my teammates as well as the coaches.

I suited up with the varsity team as a freshman. My head coach, Coach Strickland, decided to challenge me in one game. He put me in at nose guard. For people who don't know football, a nose guard is a defensive lineman who is typically a big guy who is difficult to move. As soon as he said my name, I ran onto the field. As a freshman, I was a gigantic 5 ft 2inches tall and weighed 105lbs. I was going up against a center who laughed when I came onto the field. He was a hell of an athlete, 6 ft 2 inches and 260 lbs. I don't blame the guy for laughing at me. We took our spots. I had made up my mind I was going to put this guy on his ass. I remember this like it was yesterday. I don't remember the quarterback yelling hut or anything like that. I remember that ball moving, and I jumped forward as quickly as I could. I went to the right.

My speed was my advantage, and by God, I was going to use it. I hit the center in the lower left side of his chest, pushed him back, and got a glimpse of the running back. I tried to go for the running back, but my short-lived advantage had been spent. I was now being shoved sideways by the center. The running back cut to my left. I dropped to the ground and spun using my speed one more time so I could get free and meet the running back in the hole. I was able to grab the leg of the running back. I probably looked like an ankle-biter to everyone in the stands. This gave time for our middle linebacker to clean up the tackle. After the tackle, I remember catching my breath and standing up. I got a tap on the helmet by one of the guys.

Then it was time for the next down. I took my spot. Now the center was not laughing at me. He looked pissed. Now he knew I wasn't scared. We looked at each. The center hiked the ball. This time, the center was expecting my quick burst forward. He could counter by stepping back quickly instead of moving forward initially. He took his massive paw and caught me in the chest. It stopped me in my tracks. I was then being shoved back away from the play. I saw the play, but it was going away from me. I was not a factor in this play now. I did okay for my first two plays on the varsity team. From that point on, my coach decided that I could play, but I didn't play anymore that night. He pulled me from nose guard back to the sideline. But the groundwork was set for me to get some playing time in the future. I did start getting playing time on special teams from then on.

I ended my football career as an outside linebacker, weighing a massive 120lbs and a staggering 5ft 4inches tall. I still had the same mentality of "my heart is bigger than yours." "You hit me and I will hit you harder". "I will not be put in a box; I will break that damn thing". This served me well in my weight-lifting career, which happened entirely by chance.

One day, Coach Strickland came into the weight room and asked me if I wanted to compete in weightlifting. I had never competed in weight lifting before. He said that I should be able to place in the state weightlifting tournament. I would have to start deadlifting to practice. Part of why he asked is that I bench-pressed and squatted all the time with people much heavier than I was. I was lifting the same weight as some of our linemen on the football team. I enjoyed bench press, lifting more than double my body weight. I also enjoyed squatting and lifting almost 3 times my body weight. Coach Strickland advised me to go to a regional weightlifting competition. I didn't even know how to deadlift properly at that point.

I thought about it for a few seconds and decided. Yes, I would go and compete. In my mind, I thought, "What could it hurt? I get to be out of school for a day and compete". I had to compete at the regional meet to qualify for the state tournament. On the way to the regional meet, Coach advised me to do lifts at a weight we knew I could do for the first set. In weightlifting, you get three lifts; the strategy is to increase the weight with each. The first lift, you want a weight you're sure you can get. The second lift you try is close to your personal record. Then, in the third lift, you try to exceed your personal record.

Once we got to the regional competition, only two days after he asked me if I wanted to compete. He took me and the other two people competing to the side and showed us how to deadlift for a competition properly. I started with the bar to make sure I could do it correctly, then I started adding weight. I got a good idea about where my strength was. Then we went to regionals with two days' notice. I did not cut any weight at the time or know the weight classes. As a sophomore, I weighed 110 pounds, showed up, and made weight without any issue. The lightest weight class is 123 pounds. We started with squats as our first lift. This made me happy as it was my favorite lift. I put 225 on the bar and was able to lift it easily. I looked at the judge, and he said, "Not a good lift! I was confused. I asked, "Did I not go low enough"? He advised me that I had a pager on my hip, which was against the rules. I informed him it was an insulin pump and that I needed it to stay alive. He looked at the device and realized it was an insulin pump. He changed his ruling to, yes, that was a good lift. It was the first time he had seen a device like that. He was not used to diabetics competing, like many people from where I grew up.

Then the second lift for the squat came around. I put on 265 pounds. I lifted it with ease. The same judge gave me the thumbs up. It was a good lift. After the second lift, I realized there was a way to keep track of who was winning per weight class. I looked at it and I was on top. One kid behind me was within 20 pounds of the weight I had just squatted. So, then I realized needed to add more weight for the third lift. I decided to go 5 pounds over my best weight at that time, to 280 pounds. I knew my adrenaline was going, and I could probably get more weight today. I ended up getting my third lift with ease as well.

I looked at the standings. Now I was 50 pounds ahead of the next closest person. I got excited. The next lift was a bench. I knew I would do well in this competition. I ended up adding another 20 pounds to my lead. Then came deadlift. I had never maxed deadlift. I had no clue where I topped out at. I knew I could get 225 just from practicing earlier that day. So that's what I started with. This was the only lift I was nervous about. It seems so simple. You pick up the weight when advised to pick it up and put it down. You do this without letting the bar go down during the lift, which is called a hitch. It's got to be a smooth, steady pull to your waist. Looking back now, yes, it is the easiest lift. However, this lift was foreign to me.

As I took my position to do the first lift, I realized that most of the people I was competing against had already lifted. This meant I was trying to lift a heavier weight than most competitors. Only two of my competitors were lifting more or the same as me. I got the command to lift the weight. The weight shot up off the ground, then went straight to my waist. I looked at the judge, who gave me the okay to put the weight down. As I walked by the judge, he said, "That weight is way too easy for you". Then another coach from another school stopped me and asked if I had ever deadlifted. I advised him, "No, this is my first time competing. I didn't know about deadlifting until today". He took me to the side and showed me how to set my feet properly and grab the bar to get the most leverage. He told me I looked goofy up there trying to lift, but I had enough strength to pick up the 225-pound weight. Doing these few things should make me more stable and able to lift more. He advised me that he did not want me to hurt myself once I got to a heavier weight.

After chatting with this coach for a few seconds, I looked at the standings for my weight class. My 70-pound lead had been whittled down to 30 pounds. I decided then and there to use my squat lift as a comparison. I jumped up to 275 pounds. I hoped I had not bitten off more than I could chew by jumping up that high. Taking advice from the coach and watching other competitors lift, I realized I needed to put one hand underneath the bar, and one hand on top of the bar, spread my legs a little bit more, and lift more with my legs and less with my back. I practiced my hand grip and spread my legs between competition lifts. I did feel more stable, and it felt more natural. Then it was my time to get up on the stage and lift 275 pounds, that is a lot of weight for a 110-pound individual to lift. I grabbed the bar appropriately and lifted as the judge gave me the sign to lift the weight. Surprisingly, the weight came off the ground just as easily as the 225 pounds. I was excited again. I had the belief that I could win now.

By this time, I'd realized who my competition was, and they were creeping up closer to me. I had added a few pounds back to my lead. I now lead by 35 pounds going into the final lift of the competition. The person I was lifting against decided they would lift 35 pounds heavier than I initially put down. Then, just before my lift, I switched my weight to equal their weight. I would win this competition outright by tying him in deadlift or lose the lift entirely. Because I had won the bench press and squat lifts, I was going to state either way. In retrospect, this was not a very smart move. I was already advancing, so the only reason to try to outlift my competition in deadlift was ego.

Since I was the last to change my weight, I went after him. He lifted his weight, but he hitched halfway up. This meant his lift was no good. I went up after him, knowing I had already won the competition. This lift was just for me. It was 315 pounds. I looked at the judge who raised his arm, signaling me to lift the weight. I pulled with as much strength as possible, and the weight slowly started to come off the platform. I had not felt that much pull in my stomach and legs before. I could feel the blood rushing to my head. It felt like my eyes had a ton of pressure behind them. Slowly, that weight kept coming up. The weight made it to my waist. The excitement of what I had just done took over. I dropped weight. I had lifted more weight that day than I had ever lifted before. I did this as a sophomore! As I looked at the judge after I dropped the weight, he said, "No lift". It didn't count because he had not commanded me to drop the weight. My excitement turned to dread because I did not do my best. However, I did do enough to win the regional competition. My coach came up and congratulated me, as well as the other guys I was competing against. Several asked where I came from and how I could lift that much on my first time lifting. I'm not sure about anything other than all the farm work and hay hauling. It had set me up perfectly for this. My arms and legs were conditioned for the abuse of lifting heavy things.

After the competition, when I received my medal for winning, the guy who came in second place approached me. He stated, "It was supposed to be my year to win state". He had come in second the two previous years. Now, I came out of nowhere to be his main competition. He was mad that his coach helped me with my form. Then he said he was glad to have competition. The closest person to us was 60 pounds behind us. We had run away from the competition. This was my first weightlifting competition, and it was by far the scariest. I'm glad I took the leap of faith and listened to my coach about competing. I also had to learn on the fly and watch other people. I was definitely outside of my comfort zone on this one. The two other guys who went with me from my school also did okay. We were all sophomores. Little did we know that we would be the start of a great weightlifting program at Bray-Doyle, Oklahoma. I ended my high-school career with three individual state championship titles in weightlifting. I also led the team to our first-ever championship title in weightlifting in my senior year. I did that by winning every lift that year for my weight class.

Never let anyone or anything steal that fire in your heart to be the best at what you do. So, what if you do not fit in with "society's norms"? That is okay!! It just means you are made for something more than usual. Be excellent at whatever you do; if this upsets people, that is OKAY. I made the mistake of trying to fit in for many years. It was not until I broke away from the people who kept telling me "Always remember who you are, you are just a small country kid", and "don't forget us small people." These are just ways for people to steal your desire to be great. It is almost like blackmailing you into their thinking and making you feel bad for wanting more in life than they do. Think big and do not be ashamed of it. You owe it to the world and to your family to be the best version of you possible.

Some of the most successful or smartest people in the world have overcome many obstacles in their lives. Look at Stephen Hawking, Elon Musk, Stevie Wonder, Ludwig van Beethoven, and Abraham Lincoln, to name a few. These people had a wide range of disabilities/challenges in life. They showed us that if we keep pushing through and never take our eyes off the target, we can achieve greatness. This can happen if you focus your efforts on the right things. All it takes is that initial first step to get you rolling in the right direction. My first obstacle was that diabetes made my life harder. So what? I will not let that define me.

I want people to think of me as a successful person, not a victim of circumstances. I encourage the reader to reflect on their life and decide what could hold them back. Face it head-on. It could be family problems, financial issues, addictions, illness/disability, where you live, or something else. Find people who have done what you want and get their advice. People are willing to help if you show the initiative. Take that first step to get what is yours; do not wait until your time has passed. Get up and start moving to achieve your goals today, not tomorrow. Do it today; there is no guarantee you will have tomorrow. If you wait until tomorrow, you risk never starting.

Life Lessons

1.   Do not let circumstances define you. You are better than you are in your current situation.
2.   Keep getting up. Life isn't about how hard you can hit, but how hard you can get hit and keep getting back up. (Rocky)
3.   Make it a competition to prove people wrong about you. Use haters as motivation.

Questions for the Reader

1. What would you do in life if you could not fail?

     _____

     _____

2. What motivates you?

     _____

     _____

3. What is a box that people have you in that you want to break out of?

     _____

     _____

4. What is your main takeaway from this chapter?

     _____

     _____

Chapter 5

Stay Positive,

Keep Moving Forward

Even after the worst situations, a lesson can always be learned. Since first grade, I did not like school. I would try to find ways to avoid class. It was with reading that I struggled the most. I was one of the children labeled with a reading disability. I could not read like everyone else. I would invert words, sentences, and even whole paragraphs. It was like trying to read but the phrase kept wriggling randomly on the page. I would try to fill in words to make things make sense. However, this resulted in people laughing at me when I read out loud in class. I was embarrassed and never wanted to be called on to read in class. I would try to hide in the corner and be invisible. I even faked bathroom emergencies as much as I could get by with. I had a teacher didn't know what to do with me. They just labeled me dumb and moved on to the normal kids. Unfortunately, that label followed me.

In elementary school, I was placed in special ed classes because I struggled to read, but I never received a diagnosis or specialized help. I had to teach myself to read because I was not getting much help from school or home. We did not have a true special ed program so the resources were limited. I had to repeat things 10-20 times to make things stick. I would read the lessons before class multiple times. I became very good at listening to lectures. I adapted to the situation. I made it out of the special ed class by high school. I was one of the best students going into high school. I graduated from high school with a 3.87 GPA. In College, I could adapt again and do well in school. In high school and college, I had pushed through by putting my nose down in a book, locking myself in a closet, and grinding until I understood the topic while the letters danced across the page. Applying to medical school, things had to change. I had struggled with standardized tests my whole life. The MCAT (Medical College Admissions Test) would be no different. The timed tests would frustrate me, and the words would start dancing on the page or computer screen. After venting to a few other people about this, I was advised that I may have dyslexia. After being labeled with diabetes, I damn sure didn't want another label. But I also needed help. I finally took this to my PCP (primary care physician), and they diagnosed me with dyslexia. Once I had the diagnosis, I was able to start working on a plan to fix the problem.

I knew I had to re-learn to read after I was formally diagnosed with dyslexia in college, but I didn't know where to start. My then-girlfriend-now-wife's father is a physician and pointed me in the right direction. I needed visual/speech therapy. This is not cheap. I was working 3 jobs and going to college at that time. I was paying for school, rent, and food. I had no extra money. My soon-to-be in-laws saw a guy with internal drive and potential to make a good doctor, and they wanted to help. They offered financial support for the dyslexia reading classes. I fought it for a little bit. I retook the MCAT and scored low again.

After getting a low score for the third time, I had to take a long, hard look in the mirror and swallow my pride. I took my soon-to-be in-laws up on the offer to help with the therapy classes' cost. This was a hard pill for me to swallow.

I felt like an idiot the first day in therapy. I was the oldest one there for treatment by a lot. It was like being back in elementary school's special education reading classes again. On more than one occasion, I had to fight the urge to get up and leave. If it had only been my money, I probably would have left. Since it was my soon-to-be father-in-law's money, I felt obligated to stay and to go back. After the 3rd session, we found things that helped. I was able to read and comprehend the first time through a story. This was different! It was almost enjoyable. I don't think I will ever read for just fun. But my comprehension and speed reading shot way up. I knew the next step was retaking the MCAT.

The fourth and final time I took the MCAT, I would love to say everything went great and I blew through it without problems, but, as you may expect at this point, that was not the case. It wouldn't be my style. I got to the testing center and started my normal freak-out in the truck before entering. I was anxious as could be. I knew this was most likely my last time taking this test. Once the test started, I forgot all the training I had just undergone. I constantly looked at the timer, getting more anxious as time ticked away. After about 20 minutes, I managed to stop myself from spiraling out of control. I had a very clear moment of telling myself, "You've done this shit 3 times already, this freaking out shit does not work". I started using the techniques I got from therapy; things were a little smoother. After finishing the test, this time before time ran out, I had to wait to see how I had done. Several weeks passed before I received the email stating my MCAT score had been posted. I was nervous as hell to look at that score. The minimum score needed to apply to medical school was over 20. The highest score I received thus far was 17. I was just as nervous logging in to look at the score as I was on the test day. I clicked the button to review my score and sat there with my eyes closed. It seemed like an eternity before I was able to open my eyes. I was relieved by what I saw. My score was 22!!!! In that moment, I knew that I would be successful. I knew if I got an interview, I would have a good chance at getting in. Now I had finally met the requirements for applying. On paper, I was mediocre at best. However, in person, I became a well-rounded student with many real-world life experiences and challenges that set me apart from other applicants. I communicate very well with people face-to-face. The gift of gab is one of the many blessings I received from my grandfather.

I have learned over the years that if you keep pushing forward or moving in some way, you will end up where you are supposed to be. Setting still and doing nothing is the worst thing anyone can do. I have seen many good people in my life who stop moving due to some category of circumstance. This leads them into a spiral of not doing anything and self-doubt that leads to depression, anxiety, or both. Then I've seen many of the same people try to self-medicate with alcohol or drugs. They get into the wrong crowd of people who tell them what they want to hear. They are never challenged to grow.

A person who does not grow or move forward gets further away from the person they are supposed to be. Deep down, everybody knows they are supposed to be something great and serve some purpose. If they are not living up to that standard, they resent themselves even more. As human beings, we are called to serve our fellow man somehow. If we do not listen and use the gifts that we are given, we fall into this downward spiral. Do not let this be you.

Even with all the challenges I've faced in my life. I still like to give people the benefit of the doubt. I think one of my strengths is staying positive no matter the scenario. Yes, I have been burned with this. However, I try to look for the silver lining in every situation. I always have the following questions with any setback.

- Is the setback I just went through a learning experience for me?
- What did I get out of this situation?
- Do I need to adjust my communication style? Was my preparation good, or could I have misread the situation?

These are just a few questions I asked myself after every setback, disagreement, or parting of ways with individuals in my life. There are always lessons to be learned.

Growing up, I watched a lot of traditional guy films. My favorites growing up were Rocky, Rambo, Roadhouse, and Tombstone, my all-time favorite. I learned lessons from these films. I learned that you need to be in shape all the time. I also learned, particularly from Roadhouse, *"just be nice"*! Even when I disagree with someone, I try to stay nice. This is a skill that I have learned over the years. I remember being a teenager and a young adult who was as hotheaded as hell. I could not keep my cool during disputes most of the time. However, with years of practice, now I can still be nice. I have come to notice that my perspective is not the only one. I try to treat people as I would want to be treated during these disputes. I understand that I make mistakes and other people make mistakes. We are all fallible people. With this knowledge, I try to be courteous and stay positive and friendly. That said, sometimes you need to know when to draw the line and stand up for yourself or what is right.

I recently had a conversation with my children. They ask, "When should we stop being nice?". My response to them was: "That's a great question. Never let someone disrespect you or anyone else. Never let someone try to intimidate you or anyone else. These are the points you should not be nice anymore". They looked at me, puzzled. I then simplified it to not letting anyone hit, push, yell, or make you sad or scared. They got it then. They said, "Yes, Daddy". Of course, the next question was what to do. "Get mommy or daddy if you can, or deal with it yourselves". They both understood then. Today, even adults have been brainwashed into believing that any conflict is bad. Sometimes conflict is needed. There are bullies everywhere, and if you don't stand up for yourself, why should anyone else? Boundaries are a great thing.

The primary purpose of boundaries is to protect yourself. By defining what is acceptable and unacceptable to you, you protect your personal well-being and create healthy, balanced relationships. Boundaries foster a sense of safety, respect, and trust, allowing you to maintain your emotional energy, avoid burnout, and live more authentically by prioritizing your own needs and values. I have included two quotes explaining why you need boundaries, followed by two quotes about implementing boundaries in your life.

"When we fail to set boundaries and hold people accountable, we feel used and mistreated. This is why we sometimes attack who they are, which is far more hurtful than addressing a behavior or a choice."

– Brené Brown, "*The Gifts of Imperfection*"

"You are in control of your life. Set new boundaries by removing all of the toxic people from your inner circle."

– Germany Kent

"If someone is inconsiderate or rude to you, risk telling them how it made you feel or that you didn't appreciate being treated that way. If you tend to talk yourself out of anger by telling yourself that you don't want to make waves, try telling yourself instead that it is okay to make waves sometimes and risk letting people know how you really feel."

– Beverly Engel, "*The Nice Girl Syndrome: Stop Being Manipulated and Abused — And Start Standing Up for Yourself*"

"The more you value yourself, the healthier your boundaries are."

Lorraine Nilon, *"Spirituality, Evolution and Awakened Consciousness: Getting Real About Soul Maturity and Spiritual Growth"*

My advice to people is to know what lines you're not willing to let people cross. Please stand up for yourself because it is up to you to set your boundaries. If you're not assertive with your boundaries, the person who disrupts your peace will most likely continue to do so. Communicate clearly with them about the boundaries. Always keep in mind the relationship you have with a person. With close friends and family, the boundaries can be more relaxed. However, in a professional setting, the boundaries must be very clear.

Despite what the news says daily, there are still good people in this world who are willing to help you succeed. But always be on the lookout for the people who only do things for themselves. I understand this isn't easy. I've had my share of people who have taken advantage of me. The trick is not to let it get you down and defeat you, but to see it for what it is and move on. It is typically a lesson that you need to learn to be successful. You will keep repeating the same mistakes until you prove that you understood the lesson you were meant to learn.

Life Lessons

1. Always remember that you are capable of great things. Keep pushing forward.

2. Be willing to set boundaries with anyone.

3. Never doubt the importance of friends and community in helping you.

Questions for the Reader

1. List five boundaries you have.

    _____

    _____

2. Is there someone you need to set boundaries with?

    _____

    _____

3. What's the main takeaway from this chapter?

    _____

    _____

Chapter 6

Medical School

I made it to medical school!! I soon learned that medical school was a different type of beast. We started with a "quick refresher" of all undergraduate science material in 2 weeks. I did well with that. Then the new material started. I was drowning, barely keeping my head up, it seemed like. The amount of information we, the medical students, had to cram into our heads daily was like drinking water from a fire hydrant. We were constantly running on the hopes and dreams of one day being able to help someone. That and the insane amount of coffee we were consuming at that point. I would focus on the next test or whatever hoop the school mandated us to do that day.

Our school had just switched to a systems-based curriculum from the traditional subject-based curriculum. This sounds great, learning everything you need to know about anatomy, histology, physiology, pathology, and basic management for each system, like pulmonology or cardiology. You can focus on that one system and master how everything works together simultaneously. However, being the first class to transition in anything significantly is difficult. Some professors were mad about the switch and did not change their lectures to match the new curriculum. I am sure you have heard the saying "Shit runs downhill". As medical students, we were in the valley catching most of it, as you can imagine, in a curriculum designed to teach the big-picture-down, with some people still teaching minutia-up, the system foundation crumbles.

Some professors were bitter at the change and inadvertently took it out on us. Hell, I felt lucky just to be there. I wasn't going to complain. I think most of us felt the same at the beginning. I was rolling with the punches. I was putting my head down and pushing through- like always. Many days, I locked myself in my studio apartment and unplugged all the potential distractions. I got into medical school knowing it would be hard and stressful, and it certainly didn't disappoint.

Finally, after the first few months, we realized we were severely behind in our education. We learned that the system approach was a good idea, just not being executed correctly. We were not being taught how the systems or subjects actually worked together. The broader understanding of the human body was missing from the lectures. We did our best to explain the problem to the administration. I am sure our class president won some grey hairs for his efforts in trying to convey our concerns. However, it wasn't until we started taking assigned COMLEX questions (prep questions for our board exams) that administrators realized there was a problem. As a class, we were scoring well below average in broader concepts. Administration started to pay more attention to the lectures.

As always, in bigger organizations, change is a very slow process. My classmates and I realized that we were going to have to go the extra mile to teach ourselves the missing concepts until the administration got things fixed. We made study groups. We taught each other. We made lasting connections with many people in medical school from all different social backgrounds. A lot of my classmates would do anything to help if they could. As a group, our different strengths helped each other master the broader concepts that we were not being taught.

Our class had a mix of people from various educational backgrounds, too. Some came from hands-on, direct patient-care backgrounds, such as former EMTs, lab techs, and nurses. We even had a few former chiropractors. Others came from more laboratory or research-based backgrounds. All of us together made one hell of a team. There was one girl in particular in our class who was always so sweet. She made flash cards and study guides for the whole class; they were still using her study guides two years after us- they were that good. Most of us knew there was a chance in the future we could be responsible for saving each other or a family member's life. So, we wanted everyone to know the correct information.

As with any type-A, competitive group, my class did have the occasional gunner. A gunner is a person who does not always give you correct information so they can be at the top of the class. They were identified quickly and had to study by themselves.

Even as hard as the science and medical aspects of school were, I was still happy to be there and learn how the human body works. I was frustrated with some of the extra challenges, but in the end, it was all still relevant. We all had a few brief times when one of us needed to vent some annoyances to each other. We would have our blow-up and get back to work. We knew the next no matter what, a round of tests was coming. We learned to lean on each other and listen. We encouraged each other when needed. Medical school doesn't care how smart you think you are; it will humble you.

With all the support from each other, we kept pushing ourselves to new limits. We all had a caring or gentle spirit in one way or another. Even with our generally low-key demeanors, there was something that just pissed us all off in my medical school; it was a class called "Introduction to the Patient". This class was headed by PhDs who had never even treated patients. We had many lectures/guest speakers on things like white privilege. This was at the height of DEI (diversity, equity, and inclusion). We were told several times that the only reason white people were in this class is that we somehow personally exploited other groups of people. We were also told that being white and God-forbid male was basically the equivalent of sin. Once or twice wouldn't have been so bad, but they beat us over the head with it for a whole semester. You may be shocked to know that with a name like "introduction to the patient," we never met a damn patient. Then again, if you met the professors who designed the class, maybe you wouldn't be. We students affectionately called it the "Hippy Dippy Class". We all knew this was a complete waste of our time.

After the first semester and many complaints, they calmed down on the white privilege stuff and switched to income disparity. Again, it was people who had never lived hard times teaching what they think the world is like for those in poverty. This WILL piss off people who have lived it. They turned my lived experience of childhood food insecurity and hunger into childish games and forced us to play them. If we didn't play along, we got threatened with possibly getting kicked out of school. Yes, that is right, not failing class or having a track record of being disrespectful, but simply saying you don't want to play a made-up game could get you kicked out of medical school when I was there.

I finally snapped one day when they wanted us to put rocks in our shoes to walk around and experience what Diabetic Neuropathy would feel like. As a diabetic trying to protect my feet to avoid ACTUAL diabetic neuropathy, I wasn't going to do it. I did get in trouble, but they decided against pushing to remove me because they knew they were wrong. In theory, the class was meant to build empathy for patients and other healthcare workers who were not physicians. I can confidently say that for most of my class, it only fostered resentment of the class itself. We learned far more empathy from simply being around each other, learning from each other, and struggling through the whirlwind that was medical school than that class could ever have begun to impart.

Medical school definitely had its cons, but it had pros too. Minus the few examples previously mentioned, most of the professors and doctors teaching us were great individuals. I fell in love with OMT (Osteopathic Manipulative Treatment). When I was a first-year student, I had a few mentors from the second-year class. The funniest one was the Jolly Green Giant. This guy was 6ft 7 inches and had an attitude as well. He was an OMT teaching assistant who was very good at OMT. He and some of the physicians who helped teach actually helped correct my back pain by using OMT. I liked the hands-on approach to medicine; this brought me back to my roots of working with my hands to fix the problem. I liked the idea of helping patients without medications. I liked that when done properly, there is little to no downside of OMT. I always took the original teachings of A.T. Still (the father of

Osteopathic Medicine) to heart. He did not like medications. His teachings were to correct misalignments of fascia, muscle, and bones to restore blood flow. He was also very concerned with nutrition. These philosophical differences are one of the main reasons I chose a DO school over a traditional MD school. I have included the four tenets of osteopathic medicine.

1. **The Body is a Unit:** The body, mind, and spirit are interconnected and function as a whole.

2. **The Body is Capable of Self-Regulation, Self-Healing, and Health Maintenance:** The body has an inherent ability to heal itself and maintain health.

3. **Structure and Function are Reciprocally Interrelated:** The body's structure (bones, muscles, organs) affects how it functions, and vice versa.

4. **Rational Treatment is Based Upon an Understanding of the Basic Principles of Body Unity, Self-Regulation, and the Interrelationship of Structure and Function:** Osteopathic treatment aims to restore the body's natural ability to heal by addressing structural imbalances and supporting the body's self-healing mechanisms.

The OMT class was a reprieve from the standard book work during years 1 & 2 of medical school. A lot of us looked forward to being in that class. It wasn't just getting away from the books for a while. We got to work on each other during lab. They were the first medical techniques that we were able to use. This was amazing! I got to start using these techniques on family members, and they loved it.

They reported the benefits of the treatments. I finally began to feel like a real doctor.

Another benefit of the OMT class was that we got to work with physicians who were already practicing in the area. They were all invaluable and encouraging. They remembered being where we were and treated us like future colleagues. They would even give treatments after class. My favorite physician-teachers came from the OMT classes. They were down-to-earth people. They didn't have a stick up their bum like some other specialties. We have all had experience with a physician who seems to have a stick up their bum. They want to make everyone feel bad for asking things or not agreeing 100% with them. Maybe it was my life experience, but I didn't do well with egotistical people. I still don't. I did have to learn how to deal with them to get through medical school, though.

The first 2 years of medical school are bookwork and getting the basic skills down. Then, it is off to rotations, where we work with residents and attendings. Attendings are physicians who have completed residency training; they are the ones we all want to be one day. I remember the first rotations as if they were yesterday. I did the Rural Medical Track to return to a smaller community. This made me work a lot with physicians in rural areas. These attendings were great. They treated me as a colleague instead of a student. I got to work a lot one-on-one with these attendings. This meant that I was the first assistant on many procedures and spent more time with patients than my other classmates, who did the traditional route of going to bigger teaching hospitals. I didn't have to fight with residents and other students for procedures. This was great for me since I liked to do procedures and was good with my hands. Just one example, I had caught more deliveries than my wife, who wanted to do OB/GYN in medical school, by graduation. She even spent three extra months in OB/GYN, which I did not do.

The OB/GYN that I worked with was very chill. He asked if I had any experience with deliveries. My response amused him. "I have pulled many calves and pigs on the farm". He chuckled and, like a timer, his phone rang. He answered the phone. All he said was "talk to me". A few seconds passed; he hung up the phone and said, "Get in the truck. You are going to deliver a baby now". I immediately started to sweat bullets. I was joking, but now I'm going to deliver a baby. We drove fast to the hospital. He just sat in the seat calmly listening to music on the way to the hospital. I was a little less nervous after seeing his demeanor.

We got to the hospital, and he walked in quickly with his scrubs on. This attending very much looked like Grizzly Adams. He had a full beard, muscular build, and giant paws for hands. Hell, I think he even walked like a bear. He was a former competitive weightlifter who still enjoyed lifting heavy weights. On the way to the delivery room in the hospital, he looked over and said, "You will want to gown up". We got to the delivery room, and the nurses immediately put a gown on him and handed me one. When we walked into the room, the patient was ready to deliver at that moment. There was a stool positioned in front of the patient. I stood back. My attending grabbed me on the shoulder and set me down on the stool. He looked at the patient and said that I was a medical student who would be catching her child, and he was going to be helping. The patient agreed. What seemed like forever was only 30 seconds to maybe a minute, then the baby's head was coming out at me. I put my hand directly underneath the child's head. My attending, who was helping me, placed his hand under my hand. Then he placed his massive right paw on the child's head and said, " We have to push down slightly to get the shoulder out.

He applied steady pressure on the child's head, and the shoulder popped out immediately. He then started pushing up on my bottom hand to get the other shoulder out. I was so intrigued by the moment the child slipped out of the birth canal and into my arms. He handed me the suction. I suctioned out the infant's mouth and nose. The child immediately started crying. It seemed like I was holding the child for a long time. He worked on getting the cord cut by the father of the child. Then we placed the child on the mother's chest. The last thing was the delivery of the placenta.

Once the placenta was delivered, we made sure that there were no tears and both mom and baby were good. After everything was done, the attending looked at me and said, "Good job, doctor". I was so excited in that moment. I had waited for years to hear those words. The words had come from a well-respected OB/GYN in the community. He was a classic old-school doctor who gave compliments when they were deserved. This attending would also tell you if you were slacking. He advised me that some residents would not jump in like I did. In my mind, I was thinking I did not jump in; rather, I was thrown into the chair. However, it happened. I was able to help with my first human delivery. It was great!! Just writing this experience now, I'm still excited that I was able to be a part of that delivery. Even though I do not want to be an OB/GYN, it was my first procedure with a real patient.

The last 2 years of medical school were far more enjoyable than the first 2 years. I could finally put what I had learned in the books to use. I was getting to see patients. I would be with an attending for a month at a time. By the end of the month, most attendings would let me act as though I was calling the shots. I could present the patients to the attending and give my plan. They would think about the plan and then accept it, modify the plan, or change it completely. I was becoming more and more confident by the day. Then, at the end of my 4th year, I found out I would be going to a Family Medicine Residency. I had chosen to do family medicine because I wanted to get to know people and develop relationships with my patients. I had wanted to do ER the whole way through medical school, and then after audition rotations, I realized I was sitting there watching the clock, waiting for the shift to end. I was getting tired of seeing people at their worst all the time. I realized the ER is just a treat-them and street-them job. The only patients that you start to know are the frequent fliers. Most of the frequent fliers were at the very end stage of life, untreated psychotic patients, or addicts. I decided that I wanted to help prevent problems rather than place a bandage on a major issue. I have great respect for ER physicians. It is a chaotic world that they thrive in. It was not for me, as much as I wanted it to be.

Once I figured out exactly where I would be for the next three years of my life after graduation, I started to coast. All the tests, requirements, and rotations were coming to a close. I was starting to feel the weight of medical school come off my shoulders. I was able to finally stop cramming for a test or a rotation. I started to think about what life would be like after school.

Life Lessons

1. No matter your choice in life, there will be challenges. Be prepared to overcome them.
2. Struggles are easier to deal with as a group. The lone wolf thing doesn't work with difficult tasks.
3. Be willing to accept compliments from other people.

Questions for the Reader

1. Are you always looking to the next step before you are happy?

    _____

    _____

2. When was the last time you received a compliment? Did you accept it or shrug it off?

    _____

    _____

3. What is your key takeaway from this chapter?

    _____

    _____

Chapter 7

Graduation Day

May 14, 2017, started just like any other day. I rolled out of bed, kissed my wife on the forehead, and dressed. There was excitement in the air, the excitement of closing a chapter in my life; I was graduating from medical school today. I could say that day was an accumulation of four years of stress, anxiety, devotion, tenacity, and many sleepless nights of cramming. But it was much more than just four years; it was an accumulation of my life's journey. I was on top of the world.

My journey to graduation started many years before being accepted to the Oklahoma State College of Osteopathic Medicine. It began as a curious child who liked to play outside as much as possible. I would play for hours at a time outside. My parents let me explore. I would play with snakes, frogs, spiders, bugs, and crawdads. I was always fascinated with life. I wanted to know why and how animals were different. I wanted to learn. I spent many days watching Steve Irwin, the Crocodile Hunter, on Animal Planet.

Growing up on a farm, I got to help with the animals when it was time to give shots or catch an animal. Growing up, I helped drain abscesses on cows, pigs, and dogs. However, the most comedic was burping a cow with a water hose. If you want a good job as a child, I highly recommend being a farm kid. There are numerous benefits to this. You get very good at hands-on procedures. My hands are capable of doing things that other people could only dream of. I have excellent grip strength and can manipulate objects in tight spaces. I got this from working on fences, trucks, and tractors. All of these character-building skills raised my confidence. The confidence gained was very instrumental in my later life achievements. Let's face it, without confidence, you will not try something new or challenging.

I took the confidence I had developed on the farm with me. By then, I had had to overcome many obstacles, and it was undeniable that I was there for a purpose. This confidence and sense of purpose made me feel worthy to be in medical school. I leaned on that sense of purpose, especially at the beginning of medical school. I needed it with my past struggles in academics. Most people starting medical school do not come from the special education reading class, but I did.

Later that day, I was on stage being celebrated with the rest of my classmates. We had all gone through similar struggles to get to this achievement. Everyone who goes to medical school is challenged. Anyone reading this who thinks attending medical school is a piece of cake, I challenge you to try it. I am standing shoulder to shoulder with other individuals who gave up over a decade of their lives for education and the ability to help people. These individuals are selfless. This is the way we all start in healthcare. It is amazing to be with this group of people.

When I was standing on stage, I didn't care about all the drama that was happening before the graduation ceremony. I was unfazed by which family members were pissed off or who was sitting next to someone they did not like. My parents had just gone through their long-overdue divorce, and this was the first family event they had had to attend together. All of that family bullshit just went away. For a moment, I felt like I had accomplished something incredible. I can still remember the way I felt when my childhood doctor (Dr. Solitario) put my hood on me. She had been a constant source of support to me. By all accounts, it was her fault I was here. She never gave up on me when I was a child. She kept challenging me to go to college. She never specifically pushed me to medical school. Although she was not opposed to that idea when I mentioned it to her. It was a great feeling to be up on stage with her. I kept thinking back to the first time we met in the hospital when I was first diagnosed with type 1 diabetes. At that time, I was a scared young boy. Now I was a grown man who had graduated from medical school.

No more would I be known as just Charles Bingham. I would forever have Dr. associated with my name. Yes, I like having a doctor associated with my name. Dr. Bingham has a nice ring to it. It is one of the things we look forward to as medical students. I know this sounds arrogant, but all of us on that stage worked for that Dr. in front of our names. The word "doctor" comes from the Latin word *docere,* which means to teach. A doctor is a teacher. I teach people daily about medicine and how to improve their lives. It's no accident that physicians are called doctors.

Moments like this, where the outside noise falls away, are rare. The moments of peace, even though there is still chaos around you. I was able to hold onto this moment for about 30 minutes. I will cherish it for the rest of my life. I remember being proud of my classmates and my wife, and I remember being proud that my family showed up. I was happy for the help I had been given to achieve this goal.

It wasn't until they gave the number of applicants who had applied my year that the gravity of how rare graduating from medical school was hit my brother and the rest of my family. This was the first time they realized how hard it was to get into medical school. They didn't know that I had to beat out 4,000+ other applicants to get in the door of medical school. I knew I had changed and grown going through this crucible. I didn't know how much yet and probably never will.

I am still learning and teaching every day. Going through this has changed my life forever. I believe that is the point of these moments to help define us as individuals and change us in some way for the rest of our lives. I will never know to what degree I have changed or continue to change because of medical school.

It is my life mission to teach. I teach friends and patients how to stay fit by exercising properly. I will always be a teacher in some way or another. However, when you teach, you learn just as much. This has made me into a lifelong learner. I will constantly be looking for the next thing to set my family, my friends, and my patients up in a better situation.

Life Lessons

1. Learn to be happy with the journey, not necessarily the destination.
2. Be able to soak up essential moments. Do not let the chaos around you diminish your moment.
3. Include those that are important to you.

Questions for the Reader

1. What's your main takeaway from this chapter?

_____

_____

2. When did you let someone ruin a moment for you?

_____

_____

3. What are you willing to teach someone?

_____

_____

Chapter 8
The Fall After Success

After graduation, you feel like you're on top of the world. I had just accomplished a remarkable task. I had just graduated from Medical School. A task that few attempt and even fewer complete. And yet, a few weeks after graduation, I was lost. I was not cramming for the next test. I was not rushing to the hospital for the next rotation. I was not doing interviews, trying to get into my desired residency program. I was done with the hustle and bustle of medical school. This downtime was a foreign concept to me. Since I was young, I have never experienced a lot of downtime. I was always moving and doing something. Everyone kept telling me to relax and enjoy the moment. What the hell is this relaxing thing? I actually felt guilty for not being active. You can ask my wife; I was disoriented, and it showed. Hell, I decided I would take up guitar just for something to do. Put it this way, it was bad for anyone who was not deaf.

I kept telling myself the same fantasy I had been telling myself since high school. Once the next step is complete, I will be happy. This is a story many people tell themselves; it keeps them looking at the bigger picture in life. It is a common phenomenon among medical students as well. I thought, "once I graduate, I'll be happy". During graduation, I was very happy for a day or two. Then, a new demon sets its hooks between graduation and residency. I felt guilty waiting for residency to start. I was supposed to be helping people. I wondered if I was just a fake making it this far. I began to think I would hurt people by being a physician. This worried me greatly because I never wanted to hurt anyone. I started to look at other people and their accomplishments. I began to think they were better than I was. I even started believing in some of this bull crap for a while. I kept telling myself that once residency starts, it'll get better.

Just like thousands of medical and other professionals, I was dealing with what is known as imposter syndrome. Imposter syndrome is when you feel like you're a fraud and unable to do what you were trained to do. The definition is a psychological experience where individuals doubt their skills and accomplishments, believing they are frauds who do not deserve success, despite objective evidence. This phenomenon can lead to self-doubt, fear of exposure, and a reluctance to internalize achievements. I found out that this affects medical students, residents, attending physicians, and many other professionals. Every step along the way, you feel as though you're not prepared. It was my mind just playing tricks on me. I did communicate these concerns with my wife. She understood because she was dealing with similar thoughts. However, I had the extra weight of not being one of the strongest academic candidates. I even thought of withdrawing from residency before it started.

I went back home to Bray, Oklahoma. I needed to get grounded again. I just sat out in the pasture with the cows for a while. I walked up and down the creek banks. I realized that I needed to continue with residency. In my mind, I was scared, but I owed it to the people that I would treat in the future to put my

I set my feelings aside and became the best doctor I could. I knew that without residency training, I would not be able to accomplish this. After these thoughts, I realized I had beaten the odds thus far. I had a track record of success, no matter what was thrown at me. So, I took another leap of faith.

Once residency started, I was immediately thrown into the Medicine Rotation, where you're taking care of patients in the hospital. I worked with internal medicine physicians. This rotation started on July 1st, when interns (first-year residents) started residency nationwide. There's a running joke among healthcare workers that if you get sick, never be ill in the first few months of residency, i.e., July through September. This is when most mistakes will happen. I started my medicine rotation as a typical incoming intern, eager to help and excited to be there. I had experience as an EMT before getting into medical school, so they decided to put me in medicine first. Medicine rotation is typically one of the most complex rotations, second only to ICU rotation. Luckily, during this rotation, I would be with a senior resident. He was one of my chief residents. I will refer to him as The Fatman.

The Fatman was a great source of knowledge for me during this first rotation. It was great having the Fatman on rotation with me. He was able to help guide me in complicated patient scenarios and navigate technical issues. In addition to The Fatman, there was one other family medicine resident and several internal medicine residents on Medicine rotation. The other family medicine resident was Aaron. Aaron had completed a traditional intern year at a different facility and would be a second-year resident in our residency program. Aaron was being tested this first rotation to ensure he could supervise interns like me and be trusted to take a call at night without fearing that he would kill someone. In our residency program, the Medicine rotation consisted of 12-hour shifts, the first half of the month on days and the second half on nights.

Day rotations started going well. I was able to see the patients to whom I was assigned. Then I would present these patients to The Fatman, where he would help me with the assessment and plans for these patients. He also showed me how to work the damn computer system to put in all the orders. He also advised me on which attendings to stay clear of and how to put the orders in correctly for each individual attending. He informed me that there were a few attendings for whom the orders would be wrong no matter what you did. He joked that those are not the worst attendings. He informed Aaron and me that the worst attendings are the ones who love to hear themselves talk. Yes, we did have an attending who would make rounding last for hours. Typically, in medicine, the residents will see the patients first thing in the morning and get as many notes done and orders placed as possible. Then the next step would be presenting these patients to the attendings, usually in a group while seeing each patient (this is "rounding"). If the attending agreed with the assessment and plans, they would sign off on the orders.

The Fatman had me as prepared as possible for an intern during the patient presentations. The presentations started off painfully. It turns out that we started off with the attending who liked to make things last forever. They seemed to find joy in making us stand in the hallway. It was like they wanted to be a drill sergeant, and we were the recruits. This attending loved to make us say we didn't know. This attending found out that my weakness was the computer and zeroed in by telling The Fatman not to help me at times. The Fatman had a solution for this; we would sneak to a different area of the hospital and put in orders before this attending called us for rounds. He would show me the computer stuff a few times, and then I was alone. This was hard, but I figured it out and survived.

I soon learned that Aaron was not so lucky. The Fatman was having a difficult time with Aaron. He had to teach him about the electronic medical record computer system, just like he had to teach me. In addition, he had to help Aaron communicate effectively and help with assessment and patient plans. This was the beginning of the end for Aaron. He showed signs of weakness in his skills, knowledge, and ability to adapt.

Aaron seemed like a good enough guy. He was a little on the weird side, but nice. Hell, in medicine, most of us are "off" in some way. Aaron's weakness in patient management was a problem because he was already supposed to have one year of residency. It was like blood in the water, especially with this first attending. They rode Aaron hard for that first week. Then the attendings rotated, and we got a more seasoned attending. This attending didn't get as frustrated with Aaron. They actually taught him some. I was too busy dealing with my stuff at the time to realize exactly how far behind Aaron was. I was soon seeing more patients than he was. After discussing patients with the nighttime residents, the Fatman would decide who saw what in the morning. I was able to present these patients clearly to the attending. I was also able to avoid most of the traps during presentations. I can recall what people have told me very well. I make a mistake once, and I don't make it again. These advantages helped me avoid the traps set by attendings or self-made traps hidden in my presentations.

There is an art to presenting a patient to an attending physician. You present the facts! You state what the patient is complaining about, how long this has been going on, how bad it is, what it feels like, and if this has happened previously, etc. You then take what the patient has told you, with what you see on physical exams, as well as images and laboratory findings; then you turn this into what disease processes fit this best, and what you plan to do to treat it. Do not get stuck in the woods! If you allude to something during your presentation, you can expect to get grilled on whatever you alluded to. If you state so-called "zebras" as a possible diagnosis during a presentation, you will get grilled for the next 15-30 minutes on that diagnosis. A zebra is a disease process that happens very rarely in medicine. When you're on medicine rotation, the saying is, "if you hear hoofbeats, look for horses, not zebras". You only look for zebras when all horses have been accounted for. I kept seeing Aaron chase zebras during our medicine rotation. He kept getting eaten alive during presentations. It did not help that when questioned about zebras, he could not explain his rationale for searching for them. He was unable to keep his composure when asked as well and became combative. The attendings would all team up once you were antagonistic to another attending and would give you hell.

Since I was where I was supposed to be in my training, they didn't pick on me as much as Aaron. Aaron was getting reamed over basic science things. I was surprised; he was still getting them wrong and shutting down during the report. The Fatman tried his best to help him, but Aaron seemed mentally blocked in the hospital. I was getting the hang of the day shift when we flipped to nights in the second half of the month.

The night rotation was what everyone feared. Everyone feared the night shift because it was the residents running the hospital. The residents were in charge of the inpatient rehab, the medical-surgical floor, the critical care unit, and the intensive care units, both medical and cardiac. We also had to respond to all the issues overnight in the psychiatric floor as well as the OB/GYN floor. This scared the crap out of me. I did not feel ready to be dealing with that much responsibility. I knew I was not prepared with my knowledge at that time. My saving grace was that The Fatman would be with me and Aaron.

As expected, our first night started with me, being the intern, taking most of the admissions. Anyone who came in through the ED to be admitted, I had to see. The Fatman capped me at four admissions at a time at the beginning of the night. Then he started giving some of the admissions to Aaron. I would get four admissions, and Aaron would get maybe two. I will not lie, this pissed me off. But it is the way things are when you're an intern; you get crapped on constantly. It makes you faster at making decisions and better at quickly putting orders in and taking notes. You realize you have to hurry up and get things done, or you will stay there half the day after your night shift ends to do the notes.

It wasn't until our second night that shit really hit the fan. Again, I was doing most of the admissions. However, the Fatman got a call from the ICU saying that a patient had been extubated accidentally and needed to have a new breathing tube placed for them to be able to breathe. So, all three of us went quickly to the ICU. The patient wasn't completely extubated; however, the ball that inflated in the ET tube had deflated and would not reinflate. Therefore, air kept coming out, and the airway was not completely secured. This means the tube needed to come out and a new one placed. This is a relatively straightforward procedure if done correctly.

The Fatman initially let Aaron run this procedure. After the medication was given to paralyze the patient and keep them sedated completely, he pulled the tube. We then all watched as Aaron tried to place the new tube in this patient's airway to supply them with oxygen that they desperately needed. Aaron was not able to get the new tube placed. The patient's sats started dipping lower and lower. The Fatman was trying to help Aaron and didn't realize that the patient's oxygen level had gotten below 50%. This is a very critical level; staying at that level for too long means the patient will die. Being a former EMT, I advised him to stop trying to intubate and start bagging the patient. As soon as I said this, the Fatman looked up at me and the monitor. He then said, "OH SHIT, get a bag." I already had a bag ready and was handing it to him. The Fatman got the patient's oxygen level back up to the 90s. "Bagging" a patient is when you force air into their lungs through a mask by squeezing a bag hooked up to oxygen.

With the patient's oxygen now up, Aaron tried it again. This time, he only tried for a few seconds and said, "I can't do it". The Fatman looked at me and said, "Do it now". The Fatman started bagging again, getting the patient's oxygen level above 90%. I grabbed the laryngoscope and told them they needed to lower the table before we tried this. After the table was at my correct height, I told The Fatman to stop bagging the patient. As soon as I opened the patient's mouth, I placed the Laryngoscope and moved the tongue out of the way. I was able to see the epiglottis and the vocal cords. I advised them I needed the new ET tube, and I could place it immediately. We inflated the balloon in the ET tube and started bagging and using the ET tube. Patient's oxygen level stayed above 90 and was now stable.

The three of us went back to the on-call room. The Fatman asked me how many times I had done that. I told him I had done it a few times before medical school and several times during my fourth year. He then proceeded to question me. What went wrong? These are the words no student, resident, or attending ever wants to hear. These words mean you have done something wrong. This meant you could have hurt, put at risk, or killed a patient.

Back to The Fatman's question, "What went wrong?" Aaron started to speak, and the Farman told him to be quiet. He wanted to hear my answer. I advised him that the tube should never have been pulled without a bougie (long, plastic, bendable rod used to help with intubations) being placed down the original ET tube. The first ET tube would then be pulled, leaving the bougie in place in the airway. Then, the second ET tube could've been placed very easily over the bougie without needing a laryngoscope. This would have been less risky. The patient's airway would not have been lost completely like it had been. He said that was correct. The tube should never have been pulled without securing the airway first. He then looked at Aaron and said, "The intern just saved your butt". Aaron then admitted that he was not great at hospital procedures. The Fatman just shook his head and said, "If you are going to be a senior resident, you need to be able to do all the procedures needed to stabilize a patient overnight". I felt bad for Aaron. But I was very happy with my ability to handle the situation. That night showed me that I belonged in medicine and that my skills and decision-making ability were good.

The week did not get any easier for Aaron. He kept getting grilled during morning report. He could not paint a clear picture of the patients he admitted overnight for the incoming residents and attendings of the day shift. Morning report is the most brutal time in residency. In our residency, all the attendings for the day would come in and listen to the morning report. We would review all the patients admitted from the night before and present them on the big screen TV in the physician's lounge. The attendings and residents could see the labs and all the imaging from the night before. They would always find something we did wrong or could have done better. The residency morning report is structured like this to help you learn. If you cannot answer questions or present a clear picture of a patient's diagnosis, you will get reamed by attendings and other residents.

This was Aaron's problem. His inability to present a clear picture of the patient or give an accurate diagnosis and an appropriate treatment plan put him in the crosshairs of several attendings. It is their job to ensure residents are up to caring for patients. He was not there. It was clear he needed help with hospital services. After he was done presenting, they would move to me. I would show my patients I had seen the night before, with my history as an EMT and spending many months in the emergency department I could present a clear, concise picture of the following treatment steps. By comparison, I sounded great. The attending was so frustrated with Aaron that they forgot to point out some things I did wrong. I thought I was getting by with things. However, The Fatman put me in check the next night. He did not let me get by with much. I am glad that he did keep me in check. I needed someone to.

The illusion I had of getting by with things came to an end the following week when I had an attending, slamming his hands on a desk, yelling, and flipping over a chair because I intubated a patient in the middle of the night solo. This attendant was well known for being very short-tempered. He did not like that I had intubated one of his patients whom he had just extubated the day prior. He kept yelling and screaming that I didn't have a license yet. He also asked, "Who are you to make that call? You are a damn intern!!"

So, let's dive into the night before. The Fatman, Aaron, and I were working nights again. There had been a steady influx of patients all night. Around 01:30 in the morning, "code blue" (Respiratory or Cardiac arrest) was called overhead, meaning someone was actively trying to die. The disembodied voice gave the location as the cardiac ICU unit. One of the patients who had recently gotten a CABG (Coronary Artery Bypass Graft) started coding. By the time we got to the room, chest compressions were already in progress, and the patient was already intubated with multiple IV lines and a central line from his heart procedure. The Fatman and Aaron took over running the code in the middle of this code. There was another code blue in the medical ICU called overhead. The Fatman looked at me and told me, the intern, to go and run that code. He stayed with Aaron. When I got to the room, I faced a patient I knew minimal information about. At the shift change hand-off, I was told that he had been extubated the morning prior. The nurse quickly informed me that the patient had cerebral palsy and had been intubated multiple times over the last year.

When I got to the room, nurses were already bagging the patient. They were trying to get oxygen into the patient, but his oxygen level had dropped into the 60s despite their best efforts. It seemed like nothing was getting through. The patient's lips, hands, and feet were all blue from the hypoxia (lack of oxygen in the body tissues). A second respiratory therapist came in behind me. The first respiratory therapist was still in the cardiac ICU, working on the first code. The respiratory therapist took over bagging from the nurses and added high-flow oxygen without any improvement. I made the call to intubate the patient. We move the bed away from the wall. Pushed the appropriate medication to sedate and temporarily paralyze the patient to help with intubation. The Fatman was still working on the original code, trying to get a heartbeat back on that patient. I knew I was going to fly solo in this code. I had no time to call the attending on the phone; despite everything, the patient's oxygen was still critical, and his heart rate was slowing from the stress; we were about to lose that, too. It was up to me to save this patient; it had to happen now. Yes, you did read that right, the only attendings we had at night were on call via phone from their home. There was an ER physician downstairs, but they did not respond to inpatient situations or codes due to credentialing and hospital regulations.

As soon as the medication took effect, the patient stopped attempting to breathe completely, and I could take a look with the laryngoscope. I could see the patient's epiglottis and his vocal cords just below that. I asked for the ET tube and was handed it by the respiratory therapist. I took the ET tube from them and placed it between the vocal cords just past the balloon. Then, having the respiratory therapist inflate the balloon, we started pumping oxygen directly into the patient's lungs via the ET tube. Patient's oxygen level began to climb immediately, and his color improved. The patient's heart rate started to pick back up; even better, his danger of cardiac arrest was decreasing by the second.

As I looked around the room after intubating this patient, I realized a lot of the nurses in this room were the same nurses who were helping when I intubated the patient in the cardiac ICU the week prior. They told me, "Good job". One nurse even told me she would work a code with me anytime. I'm not sure what she meant other than she knew that I would get the job done. But it must've been comical for these seasoned nurses to see an intern run a code by himself on his second week of nights. I would love to tell you I was cool, calm, and collected the whole time. I was anything but that on the inside. My heart was racing, my knees were shaking like crazy, and I was desperately trying not to vomit in the middle of the floor. In residency, we had a saying when things would get tough and we were scared. We called it "the pucker moment". This was one hell of a pucker moment for me. It was also a growing moment. I had worked on my first code solo, and the patient was now stable because of what I did. Again, I was validated that I was in the right place.

So, back to morning report, I'm getting grilled by the same attending on call the night prior. The Fatman had tried to call this attending on the phone during the first code. However, he did not answer. Twice. We were on our own, and we knew it. This attending was questioning everything that was done the night before. He wanted to know about specific labs that "should" have been drawn before and after the patient was intubated to compare and justify the procedure. I advised him that there had not been time to obtain them. Then he wanted to know what license I was using. Let me explain, after graduating from medical school, you have a medical degree, but no license. You can apply for a license to actually practice medicine after completing your intern year. As a resident (particularly as an intern), you do it under your attending's license when you put in orders or do a procedure on a patient. He was upset because he had not approved the procedure I had done. Since this was my first code as an intern, he thought I was scared and too aggressive in intubating the patient.

I reiterated what was happening in the room before I decided to intubate the patient. I explained that I had done these before medical school residency and as an EMT. I also informed him I would do the same thing again this morning if he were in the room that I had done the night before. I then told him again that "the patient was BLUE!! I could not get the blood gas before the patient died." This statement sent a shockwave through the lounge.

This attending was so mad that he stormed out of the physician's lounge. On his way out the door, he used several expletives to describe me and the overnight team. Then, The Fatman spoke up and said I had been alone in the first place because he and Aaron were taking care of the patient from the first code. He also reminded the attending that he did not answer the phone when The Fatman called him for help. The Fatman was blaming him for not answering when he was on call. The Fatman also explained that he could not leave Aaron in a code but knew I could handle a code alone because of my previous experiences. The attending hit the door, still fuming but quiet. We didn't hear anything from him the rest of the day.

The three of us left that morning, angry that we were doing our best just to get torn apart in the report. The Fatman gave us the best words of encouragement he could. He said that both people were still alive because of what we did. Whether the attending approved of how it was done, the people who mattered were taken care of because of us. None of us wanted to be in that unsafe situation, but we were, and we had to take care of the people in front of us. The thing with residency is that hospital administrators would rather pay us, the residents, $45-50K a year working all night than pay nocturnist attendings a $275-$310K salary. We, the residents, were the cheap labor force that got the hospital received more reimbursement from the government because they were a "teaching hospital". The hospital administration could get by with our practice at night without supervision by saying we had an attending on. The attending who was onsite was in the ED, and we had an internal medicine attending on call via phone. Again, the ER docs couldn't or didn't come up when shit hit the fan, and there were several occasions where the hospitalist would not answer our calls either. So, the residents like me kept our heads down, doing our best.

The next time I was on medicine rotation, I was with a second-year resident, Lisa. I was about to learn the difference between being supervised by a good senior and a bad one. Lisa was an interesting person. She was more focused on her phone, what bar she was going to next, or what her dog was doing than what was happening in the hospital. She wanted to stay on the couch and do nothing. She figured her actions were appropriate since I was an intern and felt like she had "done her time". She did not want to take a nursing call or see admissions. Therefore, I got stuck with taking calls and admitting all the patients that came through the ED. I was holding my own for the first few days, and then that shit started getting old really quickly. Nursing call in this hospital was crazy. It was nothing to get 15-25 calls an hour. Most of the nurses were great; they had everything together when calling and had a purpose for the call. A few would call for a patient with indigestion that already had orders for indigestion medication, i.e., there was no question or problem to solve, just a time suck. Time sucks like this add up, especially when we would routinely get 12- 16 admissions per night in my intern year. Later in residency, these numbers increase to 16-20 admits a night.

I was already inching closer to my breaking point between exhaustion from switching to night shift, taking all the calls, running all the codes, and taking all the admissions. Then I had a patient come in with a G.I. Bleed. Their initial hemoglobin level was 8.5 with an INR of 2.8. INR is a blood test that tells how well a patient is clotting. When it's too high, they are at a higher risk of bleeding because they cannot create a blood clot. This patient's INR was a little over twice what is normal, and their blood count wasn't low enough to give them blood but it was low enough to be concerned. The ED admitted the patient to the Med-Surg unit since CCU was full, and they argued the patient was stable since their only complaint was fatigue. I tried to push back against the admission since the patient needed to be watched more closely than Med-Surg could provide. I ended up losing that discussion when the ED attending pulled rank. This happened a lot with a certain ED provider pulling rank and putting admits in the hospital instead of sending them to other hospitals.

Since I was forced to accept the patient, I started the admission process. The standard protocol was to stop any medications that inhibited platelets or their function of stopping blood loss. Stop these medicines to help the patient regain their platelet function and stop the bleeding on their own, or at least slow it down. I also made the patient NPO, or nothing by mouth, and started IV fluids. Their exam was normal, so they seemed well enough for the night. Then, about two and a half hours later, I received a call from the nurse saying the patient didn't feel right and had had a big bloody bowel movement. I ordered a repeat of the labs to compare to the earlier ones and laid eyes on the patient again. Her color is paler now, and her heart rate is higher. While I checked on her, the labs came back, and her hemoglobin was down to 6.2. Now she wasn't stable anymore. She was actively bleeding into her intestines and needed to be given blood. Also, more concerningly, her INR was up to 8.5. Instead of being about doubled, her INR was now 7 times higher than usual. She basically wasn't clotting at all. She had gone from being fairly stable to needing ICU. Just when I thought it was bad enough, the nurse informed me that the large IV we required to give the blood had been pulled out, and we didn't have a way to give medications.

I called the on-call attending and advised my senior resident, Lisa, about the situation. I knew that we would have to place a central line to get an adequate volume of blood, fluids, and medication into this patient quickly enough to keep them alive. We needed to give her medicine to make her clot so she had a chance to stop bleeding while also replacing her blood. Lisa didn't seem to care at all. I lost it. I was overwhelmed, drowning in admissions and phone calls, and I could see the writing on the wall that this patient was about to crash. My whole reason for being in medicine was to help and heal people, and the person who was supposed to be guiding me couldn't be bothered to get off the couch. I kicked the couch. That, at least, got her attention. I practically screamed, "I need some damn help!" I restated that the patient was about the crash. I needed some help; I needed her to get off her ass and do something. Lisa just stood there, shocked. I am sure no one talked to her that way. She started to say something, but I cut her off. I wasn't interested in excuses or a lecture on feminism and respectful tone. I told her I was behind on six patient admissions and had the emergency upstairs; either she helped, or someone was going to die. She paused for a second and decided that she would admit a patient or two while I was dealing with this central line. She didn't want to help with the emergency. I later found out that she didn't like doing procedures. I was not surprised. She didn't like doing anything. Hell, she seemed not to like anything in her life as much as she complained about it.

The attending on call happened to be the same attending who yelled and cussed me for intubating that patient earlier in the year. I explained the patient's situation in detail to make sure he understood how severe it was. He asked if I had done a central line before. I told him yes; I had done a central line before, but not alone. To my dying day, I will never forget his response, "DON'T MISS!!!" as he hung up the phone.

Don't miss? As I stood there in the hallway stunned by both my senior resident's and attending's responses I played the patient situation back in my head. This was another pucker moment.

Based on the reactions of the other people in this story, you may be thinking that I was overreacting. Let me reassure you, I was not. A central line is a big ass IV that starts in the neck and goes into the top of the heart. It has three large IVs within it, so you can run multiple interventions (blood, medication, fluids, etc.) all at the same time very quickly. The vein that we put this giant tube into sits right next to the carotid artery, and if you are not careful, you can poke the needle into the wrong one. That is always a bad day, but in a patient with an INR of 8, it's a death sentence. Ideally, we would avoid placing a central line in someone who is clotting so poorly, but because her blood volume was so low, we were struggling to get regular IVs, and she needed too many things too quickly to play around. Also, let me remind you. This was my first-ever central line that I did by myself.

To this day, that is the most cautious I have ever been putting in a central line. I was so careful that I barely stuck the needle into the vein and then started feeding the guide wire through. I verified t h a t the guide-wire was in the right vessel with ultrasound and watched the patient's ECG. You know you've taken the central line far enough when you see irregular beats on the monitor. The heart doesn't like to be tickled, and it gets a little jumpy. Once I got the central line in place, we could give the patient plenty of blood and medicine. The nurse in the room with me was terrific, by the way. After the procedure, we both had to take a moment to collect our thoughts and calm down. In the hallway, she asked why I, as an intern, had to do that for such a critical patient? I informed her of the situation, and she was astonished. She assured me the patient would be watched closely the rest of the night. The patient stabilized and survived the night. The next day, the G.I. Specialist came in and was able to clip the bleed in the patient's colon. This was a good story from what could've easily been a terrible one. I could sleep at night knowing I had stepped up when the patient needed me.

These examples of my internship show you that while life was not fun as an intern, my confidence grew with each scenario I survived, and I learned something about medicine and myself. In residency, you make lifelong friends just like in medical school. However, friendships from residency are much more intense. They were going through the same trauma that I was. We had a bond from this trauma. Our residency program got into some hot water because of the questionable decisions that the administration was making, such as having residents running the hospital without on-site supervision. We were actually threatened with being shut down. The hospital decided that they did not want our residency program anymore because of the requirements they would have to follow from the federal government. Therefore, I was in the last class to graduate from my residency program. My wife, a year behind me in the same residency program, had to graduate from a brand-new residency program (thankfully, in the same city). This is very uncommon. However, there was too much for the administration to fix, so they let it go. I did not learn how administrators worked until my senior year in residency.

During my last year, I was voted one of the chiefs of the program. I knew I did not want to be chief from watching the other chiefs during my previous two years. Every resident, attending, and administrator would call me or my co-chief to complain. I liaised between the attendings, the residents, and the administration. This was definitely a learning experience for me. I was always well-versed in saying what was on my mind, even to attendings. I didn't realize how much work was put on my previous chief residents until it was my turn to shoulder the work after other residents ran their mouths. I feel sorry for The Fatman now, as well as Durin and Disa. Durin and Disa took over as co-chiefs from The Fatman in my second year of residency. It seemed like everyone wanted to argue about something as soon as I became chief. They wanted me to help them change something. I mostly agreed with them on things that needed to be changed. However, good luck convincing the attendings or administration to change anything. Hell, I was better off talking to a damn fence post the majority of the time than trying to get administration to change. I had to pick my battles.

At the beginning of my senior year, it was obvious that I was idealistic. As chief resident, I wanted to invoke change. I would come in, even though I had little ground to stand on as a chief, and try to strong-arm a solution. This would get the discussions going, and my program director would be able to get some change started after my unconventional approach. My program director was well known for being a people pleaser. We worked well together because I would go into meetings demanding the whole galaxy. I would argue that it would be beneficial if we (the residents) controlled the galaxy, then my program director would be able to come in and settle for the moon and stars. It was a classic go in demanding everything but settling for the key things you wanted. My approach would throw the administration off guard, and they would be worried about all of the demands, and my program director could get them to agree to fix a few issues. My program director always said he knew exactly where I stood, and he never had to guess. The other thing that helped us force some change was that outside agencies were observing us at that time. They were trying to decide whether or not to pull the residency's accreditation due to mistreatment of residents and patient safety issues.

The important thing was that I got to sit in on administrative meetings. Hospital administrator is a fancy way of saying: "I find ways to get every cent out of government funding, which usually means making physicians' and all healthcare workers' lives harder". They try to get every cent, even if it pushes the boundaries or requires data manipulation. You can't have significant C. diff infection numbers (a metric used to evaluate hospitals, which ultimately affects how much hospitals are paid) if you make it impossible to order the test that looks for C. diff. I have seen this rule across multiple organizations. The numbers look fantastic, but at what cost? How many people aren't treated because the test isn't ordered when it should be? I saw firsthand how people who did not attend medical or nursing school were dictating medicine. They are basically practicing medicine without a degree. These people would not understand how to treat a patient if one fell over in front of them. Sadly, this is what medicine has become. I thought this was specific to my residency program, specific to our administrators. I was naïve.

Being a chief resident, I got to meet with other chief residents. They had very similar concerns to mine. Maybe not to the degree I had, since my residency was shutting down, but they all had doubts. When I asked what we could do about this, they looked at me, puzzled, like we couldn't do anything. This was deeply troubling for me. Here we were, the best and brightest residents with legitimate concerns and no belief that we could change anything. I left that meeting sick to my stomach.

I did not go back to my car initially. I decided to walk around the medical school where our meeting had been held. After saying goodbye to a few friends I hadn't seen in a while, I just stood there, lost. I remember looking outside at the parking lot and the trees behind it. I decided I'd walk over to them and sit for a minute. The sickness in my stomach was still there. I wondered, was that the point of medical school and residency to convince us we had no power? In medical school and residency, the saying is "shit runs downhill". The constant joke is that we're in the valley, so we are covered, and there's nothing you can do about it. That's just how medical education is. Had we been groomed into submission? Surely, I thought, it was part of the education; it would be better as an attending. I just needed to make it to being an attending, and everything would be better. I had fallen back into the mentality that the next step would make me feel better.

By now, I had only a few months left in my residency. I was counting down the days again till graduation. I was just killing time, and I took a month's vacation at the end. I did a lot of fishing, played at the lake in a kayak, and shot at the range. I was finally starting to enjoy the small things again. Catching a bass at the lake, the smell of burnt powder after shooting, working on your guns and equipment, ensuring everything is in good working order, or just floating on the lake or river. These were the things that brought me back and grounded me in reality.

With time to reflect and evaluate, I realized all the trials and tribulations of residency had made me more confident and secure in who I was. Every time I was placed in a sink-or-swim situation, it built my confidence. I would love to tell you that in every scenario I was put in, I succeeded, but that is not the case. There are a few instances throughout residency where I stumbled. The one thing I could always lean on was my proficiency in doing procedures. A farm boy can still work with his hands.

I also realized how much I had learned in residency because we, as residents, were left on our own. In my second year of residency, I had more confidence than some attendings. I could start moonlighting in urgent care because I had confidence in myself and my training. One of the attendings who was well known for abusing residents stopped targeting me after I was able to correct their procedural mishaps on multiple occasions. Even though the situation I was in sucked significantly, I became very resilient and resourceful. Looking back, I am conflicted. I learned a hell of a lot, and residency built my confidence because I was left to my own devices. But at the same time, it was unsafe and put patients at significant risk.

During the last two years of residency, I became known as the guy everyone wanted to be on the night shift with. I was the senior resident who would ensure the patient was cared for. I was not the best at teaching younger residents during the day. That was my co-chief; he was very good at slow teaching procedures. I was the one who, when life was on the line, would take over if needed. Looking back at these scenarios, I recognize that this helped address some of my imposter syndrome. Each of these situations made me realize I am a good doctor. I can be a good physician.

One of the most important things I learned in residency was how to stand up for myself and patients. Throughout my childhood and throughout medical school, I did not like verbally disagreeing with people. I preferred to silently wait and leave the situation altogether. I still don't like disagreeing with people, but now I know I have to. I have to stand up for myself when I am being disrespected. I have to stand up for patients when things are not right. I was pushed into unsafe situations by attendings and fellow residents on occasion. I quickly learned how to voice my displeasure with these situations. My interaction with Lisa was the turning point I needed. She was not the only resident with whom I disagreed, but she was the first. She is a significant part of my growth as a physician and a human being. This is why she is included in the book. I have many other examples, but she was the hardest one for me.

Throughout residency, I also found my retreat. The place that I go to re-center myself and gain clarity. Whenever I need clarity, I go to some form of nature. I need to get away from the noise of a city or town. Looking back, I've always been this way, but I didn't consciously think of it until the end of the residency trial. Whenever I face a difficult decision, I go to the woods. It is a great way to get grounded and find what I want or need to do. I encourage everyone to find their area of comfort where they can reflect.

My favorite place is in nature, watching deer in a field or cows eating in a pasture. This seems to be what calms me down. I enjoy watching these creatures do what they do naturally. Hell, half the time when I go hunting, I watch deer play. I typically see deer every time I go hunting, but I rarely pull a trigger. Sometimes I wish for their peace in living in the moment. They don't care what happened to them earlier that day. They're not looking 10 years into the future. They are focused on that moment, and they are present. In these moments, we find what is most essential to us. It is that clarity that everyone searches for. So go, find your place in nature, your point of interior stillness, and your clarity.

Life Lessons

1. Know when to stick up for yourself and others!! You also need to know how to do that!
2. Play to what you are the best at. Use the gifts God gave you to do the best you can in this world.
3. Learn to maximize the situations you are in.

Questions for the Reader

1. What are you the best in the world at?

_____

_____

2. When did you last sit and reflect on your life or situation?

_____

_____

3. What's a main takeaway from this chapter?

_____

_____

Chapter 9

The Great Deception of Healthcare

After graduating from residency, I did a brief stint working with a family residency program and OSU medical school, teaching OMT for a year. This was a great time with fellow colleagues. I thoroughly enjoyed working with the OSU-OMT department. This was one of the more relaxed jobs I've ever had. I was able to interact with students and residents consistently. I was also able to keep a patient panel. I took this job anticipating working for one or maybe two years while my wife finished her residency program. The thing about teaching is that you do not make as much money as a full-time physician seeing patients. I had almost $200,000 in debt at that time. This was only medical school debt. I was able to make it through undergrad without any debt. I worked three jobs and also had a scholarship in undergrad. I am proud to say that I graduated with no debt from undergrad. In medical school, I tried to work initially; however, with the amount of studying that was demanded of me, I was unable to work during medical school. Therefore, I had to live off student loans. A lower salary from the teaching job made the budget a little tighter than it had to be. Don't get me wrong. I took out the money. It is my job to pay it back. I just had to start looking at other options.

So, after the first year, my wife was getting ready to graduate from residency and we started looking at other employment options. We looked at several organizations in the area, and some that were closer to my wife's family. My father-in-law pushed hard for us to move to the organization that he worked for as a physician. He was actually one of the administrators. He pushed his organization hard and the fact that they marketed it as a physician-led organization was very intriguing to me and my wife. At each level, there was supposed to be a physician making the calls in the organization. We wanted physicians to be the ones making calls in healthcare. In many organizations we look at, physicians are told what to do by people who have MBAs. I wanted to work for an organization that understood some of the challenges of being a physician.

We continue to discuss options for many months. My wife and I interviewed at several different organizations. All the organizations we interviewed had a connection to the rural area. We asked different organizations, including my father-in-law's, the same question: "What would you change about your organization?" The answers from each of them were always the same. "There's not much we would change about our organization. There are a few minor things; nothing drastic." This was even the answer from my father-in-law. It seemed like a rehearsed line they all knew. I always had a sinking suspicion I was being lied to. The answers were too consistent across the different organizations that had no connections with each other.

However, I could not understand what they were lying about. Even with my father-in-law, I had that uneasy feeling when discussing his organization. My wife had this feeling about all the other organizations, but did not have that unsettled feeling about what her father told her. She voiced many times that her dad would not lie to her. I was still skeptical that his picture of the almost-perfect organization couldn't be accurate. Without being able to nail down what was happening, we signed the contract with my father-in-law's organization and moved across the country.

Once we advised the organization that we would be signing with them, they sent us the contracts. Our initial surprise was that the sign-on bonus was half of the original agreement; it was supposed to be higher since I would be working in a rural area. After speaking with the physician over recruitment on the phone, they were unable to offer that sign-on bonus anymore. That was my first red flag; they were not staying true to their word. Everything else seemed to be what was discussed between our two contracts. After voicing concern to my wife, she stated that even with this setback, the organization seemed good. We would be able to make that money up quickly. I agreed and went ahead and signed the contract.

It is an interesting time when you're a new incoming physician to an organization. It's like dating in a way during the recruitment and early sign-on phase. They tell you everything about their organization and what makes them great. They promised almost everything you, the recruit, could want. I didn't think we were asking for much. I wanted to work full-time, and my wife wanted to work 3/4 time. I wanted the ability to do procedures that I was trained in as well as do OMT in my office. The first several months were good. Then we both started to notice suspicious things. The things that we were promised had not shown up. The equipment I requested for my procedure was still not there. I kept getting told that it was delayed due to supply issues. Eventually, the truth came out. I was advised that they would not be getting them. The organization preferred that I send patients to a specialist. Also, I was limited to three OMT patients a day.

Being me, I started to push back. My initial clinic manager did not like to buck the system. She was very much a people pleaser. She almost looked scared, sending emails to her bosses to get my equipment or to change my schedule. I was asked to increase my OMT patients to six patients a day. I was prepared to compromise with four. They finally agreed to the four patients for OMT a day once they saw how serious I was. I also requested the equipment again, stating that I had the training and could save patients from having to travel an hour to go to the specialist. I should be able to treat patients in my clinic with the right equipment. I was advised I could purchase the equipment if I wished. This offer tempted me, but after discussing it with them, they said they would keep the equipment if I left. Therefore, I decided I would not purchase equipment for the organization.

The things that kept me happy were the patients and my colleagues. Again, working in healthcare, you get very close to people quickly. You understand each other, and you understand the challenges from day to day. Physicians and other healthcare providers understand the stress that comes with the job. You're responsible for people's health, and that weighs on you. I have spent many nights lying in bed awake, wondering if I made the right decisions for patients earlier that day. I think any good physician or provider does this from time to time. Most of the patients are great salt-of-the-earth people. They listened to what I had to say and would make the changes necessary to improve their health. I listened to them as well, and we made compromises if possible. This was the highlight of most of my days. I felt that I was making a difference for the patients.

After the initial honeymoon period at the job, about 6 months into working for the organization, my wife and I found out that the person responsible for getting us to sign with the organization, my father-in-law, was leaving the organization. He had flipped his stance on the organization entirely. He stated that the organization did not care about its employees and was being poorly run, mainly by MBAs. This was a hell of a blow since we had moved across the country to be there. I was furious. We had been lied to from the beginning. We were deceived into moving for my in-laws' own personal gain. My father-in-law had worked for over three years in this organization as an administrator. He knew about the shadiness of the organization prior to us getting there. This caused a hell of a rift between us as a family. I went back to my childhood, we were manipulated by the people we should have been able to trust. The worst part was not that I was deceived, but that my wife was hurt. She had convinced me to trust her father even though my instincts told me not to. This is what hurt her. She trusted her father completely. Now she sees him as an absolutely different person from the father she glorified.

Throughout this process, I learned to be very selective about who I listen to. I learned that if my instincts are telling me one thing, most likely they are correct. I had gone away from listening to my instincts for a brief time. I do like to give people the benefit of the doubt, but in dealing with my family's future? It is my decision from now on. I will listen to other people, but ultimately the decision rests on my wife's and my shoulders. This was a tough pill for both of us to swallow. It was less hard for me than it was for my wife. I grew up being manipulated. I made my peace that this was just a stepping stone to something else. I knew that I would have to continue working in this organization for some time. We had a two-year contract with the organization and were only 6 to 8 months in.

The longer I was in my father-in-law's organization, the more I noticed things that weren't discussed during onboarding or the interview process. I realized that I had very little to no control over my schedule. I soon realized that the organization, on paper, said it was against harassment of healthcare employees. Except in reality, it seemed to be okay for patients to abuse healthcare providers verbally and even threaten them with weapons. I had a patient who was seeking benzodiazepine medication who threatened me with a bowie knife because I would not give them the medication. The patient asked me if I was prepared for a bad day if I did not provide him with the medication he demanded. I was able to calm the patient down due to my history of dealing with people from childhood. He put his knife back into the leather sheath on his side. I informed him that I would need to leave the room to look at something on my desktop computer in my office. I advised the office staff, and we were able to walk the patient out calmly. It took over three months before the patient was dismissed from practice. When this was brought up to administrators, the situation was minimized. After working for the organization for two plus years, I was shown how important I was to them.

Not only was I finding out the hidden secrets within the organization but within medicine as a system as well. Physicians and patients do not choose the treatments in medicine. The ones that dictate healthcare are insurance companies and healthcare administrators. For example, even when patients have been stable for years on a medication, the insurance company can change its formulary. Now, the patient has to be switched to something completely different. Physicians can do an appeals process that eventually leads to a peer-to-peer review. However, there have been numerous times on this peer-to-peer review when I was talking to a pharmacist. I have nothing personally against pharmacists. They are smart and great people most of the time. However, they are not a peer to a physician. Pharmacists do not treat patients. They give the patient the medications that the physician has ordered. They do not have diagnostic skills or the ability to provide long-term treatment for patients.

Still, my wife and I continue to push through with all the challenges of working in a healthcare organization and the current healthcare system. We both agreed that for the patients, we would continue working. Little did we know we were losing ourselves to the system. It seems like the grooming process starts in medical school and in residency. We are continually reminded that our voice carries little weight. We are continuously tasked with more and more things daily. A recent study from the University of Chicago showed that for a family medicine physician to get everything done for patient care and to complete their in-basket tasks, it would take over 26 hours every day to stay up with the current workload and guidelines. The last time I checked, there were only 24 hours a day. The study did not consider rest or family time, basic hygiene, or relaxation. The 26 hours needed every day is just for the job. The majority of physicians are good people who want to help. They are constantly being abused. Again, we were groomed through medical school, residency, and as attendings that this abuse is OK. We are taught that our dreams do not matter. As long as the patients are seen and the in-basket is taken care of, you don't get yelled at by the administration.

Corporate physicians and other providers today are at a disadvantage in the current healthcare system. The administration or insurance tells them what they can do and how they can do it. After so long, this gets to be disheartening. Physicians give in to the system and decide this is the way it will be until retirement. It is called "learned helplessness" and happens after repeated exposure to uncontrollable adverse events. It's hard to keep fighting when you keep losing. Many physicians only work until their loans are paid back and then quit to do something different.

The current healthcare system works perfectly the way it was designed. It works perfectly for the ones it was intended for. The ones that benefit the current healthcare system are healthcare administration, board members of hospitals, pharmaceuticals, and insurance companies. The current healthcare system works perfectly if you're in one of these groups. If you notice, the people who care for the patients and the patients themselves are not on this list. Current healthcare employees are taken advantage of daily. These groups take advantage of healthcare workers' morality and deeper calling to help people. Also, physicians are tricked into immediately becoming employed by an organization and not starting their own business. They do not get the business tax breaks when they're strictly a W-2 employee. They have minimal autonomy in their practice. From day one of medical school, we were told we must work for a company because it is too hard to start our own practice. Understanding the billing or managing the money appropriately is too much work. Physicians are told this throughout medical school, residency, and even as attendings. Furthermore, we're now told by insurance we can't treat patients appropriately because it does not fit within the insurance's so-called formulary they set. We're not allowed to get the equipment to give our patients the best outcome because it's not in the budget. I will admit this is a pretty pathetic feeling for a physician. I did not sign up for this.

Even with these challenges, my wife and I stayed in this system. We remain employed with the organization even though we knew, deep down, it was taking our souls. To stay caught up with the workload, my children were suffering because I was too tired to make it to the family functions. I was unable to focus at home. I kept thinking about patient charts and things I needed to do that day or early the next day. I know I'm not alone with these concerns. My wife and many other physicians and providers also have them. Still, the great thing about being a physician is teaching patients. As a doctor, I have had numerous opportunities to help people and teach them about their health issues. I can communicate with almost everyone to a degree that they will understand. I can speak as a farmer, businessman, doctor, and mechanic.

This is probably the best tool I have. I can explain things to patients so they can understand them in multiple ways. People love to hear about things other than medicine, too. This is where the gift of gab comes in again. People also want a physician who will listen to what's important to them and do a physical exam. I have had hundreds of people come into my office who have not even had their chest listened to in years.

One patient scenario that comes to mind was a patient in their early 30s who had been feeling fatigued for over six weeks. They had seen their previous provider 3 times and were not getting any better. This patient told me their story, explaining how they always felt tired and were getting short-winded just doing simple things. Of course, as they spoke, I formed a list of the possible causes, including coronary artery disease, heart failure, lung cancer, heart arrhythmias, anemias, endocrine issues, and kidney disease, plus many more things were going through my head. Then it came time for the Physical Exam portion of the visit. The patient seemed confused when I took my stethoscope from around my neck and stepped toward them. I saw the startled look on their face. I told them I would listen to their hearts and lungs to see if I could hear anything to help figure out what was happening. The patient smiled, laughed, and responded that they had not had anyone listen to their heart and lungs in many years.

After the exam, I informed them they would get an electrocardiogram (EKG) today. I told them that their heart was not in rhythm. I asked them if they had any histories of atrial fibrillation (A-fib). They reported that they've never had any diagnosis involving their heart. I advised them it sounded like they were in A-fib at that moment, but we needed an EKG to confirm this. This could explain why they'd been feeling so tired for so long. Within a few minutes, we had the answer. Their heart had gone into a rhythm known as atrial fibrillation (A-fib). This could have been caught so easily; honestly, I was mad at the previous provider for this patient. This patient was at high risk of serious consequences now. Being in atrial fibrillation for that long increases the risk of a blood clot leading to stroke or pulmonary embolism. Also, the excess of work on the heart from not beating properly for that long is like constantly doing a stress test or equivalent to running a marathon. This patient had been dealing with this for over six weeks.

Like I said, initially, I was very mad at the previous provider for not doing a physical exam or an EKG. However, they did do lab work. They had ordered most things that needed to be ordered, minus specific heart enzymes. This was early in my career, and I still had time to listen to patients and do a thorough exam. As I progressed in my career, I learned that the longer you were in medicine, the less time you had with patients. The more administrative burdens you have placed on yourself. The daily in-basket fills up with unnecessary tasks. Just walking into the office in the morning, it is nothing to have over 150 functions in your in-basket to address between your already packed schedule. The longer you are in medicine, the more meetings you have to attend, which are completely useless 90% of the time. All these unnecessary tasks take more time from your patients and your family. The administrative responsibilities and requirements force providers to chart at home instead of charting while seeing the patients, because we only get 5 to 10 minutes with each patient at a time. I don't blame the provider as much anymore. I blame the system.

The patient underwent appropriate testing and was placed on medication to help keep them out of a fib. Initially, the medication failed. So, cardiology decided they would shock the patient's heart back into a regular rhythm after being anticoagulated for the appropriate amount of time. I came to find out that the patient really loved their energy drinks. They were consuming 4 to 5 a day. Since being diagnosed with a fib, we had a heart-to-heart conversation that they cannot do that crap anymore. The patient laughed, stating, "I never had a doctor tell me I can't do 'that kind of crap in my life'". I told them they were messing with their heart, and I did not have time to beat around the bush. I would be straightforward and tell them precisely what they needed to do. Since that day, I have adopted that approach; patients seem to love it. This patient is back to doing their regular routine, minus the energy drinks, and their heart is doing great. They have been off all medication now for over a year.

As a physician in today's world, it is an interesting time. Physicians are the scapegoats of the medical field. People are told that physicians are greedy, which is why medicine costs so much. However, the pharmaceutical companies, insurance, and hospital administrators are to blame for this, as well as the government. Yes, physicians make a good living. However, they are firmly in the middle class now. With inflation and everything else happening worldwide, physicians are middle to upper-middle-class. Rich physicians are a thing of the past. Physicians are not the only ones punished in the current healthcare system. Nurses, lab techs, and all supporting staff are mistreated as well. They are constantly understaffed and a lot of times underpaid as well. As healthcare professionals, we try our best to give the best care possible to our patients. However, there is growing evidence that we have actually been lied to by some of the studies taught in medical school. In medical school, we learn so fast that we can't look up every study. We trust that our teachers actually looked at the things we are taught. Medical schools just run with the studies and trust that information blindly at times. We have been given false information on how to treat our patients. Government studies are so slow that it most of the studies come from big pharmaceutical companies. Therefore, everything needs to be met with skepticism and carefully thought through before making patient suggestions. Sometimes, common sense should be what helps clinicians make decisions for patients. I have become very cautious with new medications and studies. This is why we have chosen to open our own clinic.

I spent over a decade in higher education, and being told what to do by someone with half the education is ludicrous. Maybe I'm old-fashioned, but medicine should be run by physicians and the patients they treat. It should not be run by so-called "bean counters." It should not be run by insurance, which is a scam to the people forced to buy it. A patient should know the cost of something before signing to receive the procedure.
Medicine in the US does need to be fixed. I think it gets fixed when patients and physicians take back control.

In our clinic, we will be offering the most up-to-date solutions and will have the ability and speed to keep up with the changes in the healthcare field. We also use a common-sense, no bullshit approach to medication, or the more PG version, we use common sense with medications. We are open to more alternative treatments. We have returned to the roots of osteopathic medicine, which AT Still started. Our main goal is to find health and get people off medication.

Starting a business has been very challenging. Finding a place to open the business was one of the most complex parts for us. With as many people moving into Tennessee, office spaces were at a premium. Once we got that under control, the next challenge was hiring the right people and listening to the right advice. The thing about business and life is that there is no one correct answer. You present a scenario to five different successful businessmen or businesswomen. You end up with a lot of varying advice options. All the strategies can work some better than others. The biggest thing I found is to stay consistent with yourself. The discipline of consistency will get you to that next level.

In my business, my primary focus is on musculoskeletal pain. This is because ever since medical school, I have been drawn to OMT treatments. What made me the happiest was treating people with OMT and fixing their pain without medication. One of my goals is to decrease the quantity of opioids in the area where I work. I also want to empower patients to take care of themselves by collaborating with me and my team. I want to help patients avoid surgery and medications as long as possible. The body has the ability to heal itself. This is the type of doctor that I've turned into.

I would much rather fix things with my hands and avoid causing patients more pain with surgeries that they may or may not need. I want to discuss things they can do to improve their health with them. Rather than rush them into the clinic for a 5- to 10-minute visit, which is what most corporate medicine physicians get. I went to medical school to help people. My calling is to treat patients. My calling is not to treat hospital administrators or insurance companies. I have decided to be the change in medicine instead of enabling the problem. Yes, physicians and nurses are to blame to a degree. We are the ones who gave them control without fighting back. Not anymore!!

Life Lessons

1. Trust your instincts!! Don't be fooled by recruiters. Their job is to sell, no matter what the cost to you.
2. Know what you want in life and why.
3. Know what you are willing to fight for.

Questions for the Reader

1. Do you know how to deal with disagreements?

   _____

   _____

2. Do you put your judgment on a situation over other people's opinions?

   _____

   _____

3. How long has it been since you did something you are good at?

   _____

   _____

4. What's a main takeaway from this chapter?

   _____

   _____

Chapter 10

Finding My Faith

Christ is Lord!! What else needs to be said?

    I am a straightforward, to-the-point kind of guy, so expanding upon this isn't easy. However, I'll go back to the beginning. I was not always a really religious guy. At best, I was a lukewarm Christian for many years and in college. I started to believe the dogma that colleges are famous for teaching, that being religious was only for people who didn't have goals or were not smart. Throughout this time, I was just being arrogant. My pride had taken over my thinking. In my mind at that time, I needed nobody and nothing for help. In reality, that could not be further from the truth.

    Growing up, I had an interesting relationship with "church". I remember going to Baptist churches as well as non-denominational churches. As we were getting ready to go to church, my mother would be screaming and cussing the whole time, threatening us about this or that. On the way to church, she would occasionally calm down. But once we got to the parking lot of the church, her demeanor would change instantly. She would become the sweetest, most caring person in front of the church people. It was like an instant switch as soon as the car door opened in the parking lot. This puzzled me as a young child. I did not understand what was going on. I did like the version of my mother in church. Nonetheless, her facade only lasted on the church grounds. Her performance was a short-lived thing.

When I was older and could drive, I went to church a few times. But the people honestly seemed fake to me. The same people who would treat others like trash during the week would raise their hands trying to be as holy as they could in the church. This led me to question why I should be here with hypocrites like this. I didn't understand. Yes, I believed there was a god, but at that time, it didn't feel right for me in places like that. I was reprimanded multiple times for just sitting in the wrong pew. People seemed to believe they owned sections within a church. This led me to have a very poor view of people within churches. I decided I would do my own thing and that as long as I was a good person, I would be okay. My mind was made up, that was what I would be doing. I would avoid churches.

Then college started, and being in the science department, many people questioned everything, which in and of itself is not wrong. Many professors just wanted to challenge us to be able to understand and defend our own positions. That's what college is for, right? However, some faculty were very vocal about their idea that there really is no religion or supernatural. It was just people needing to have a fallback plan or who were unintelligent. Their arguments were less about helping us grow and more about proving they were right. As a young adult, I started to believe some of this crap. If you get trash shoved down your throat long enough, you start to believe the garbage is food. Even in Oklahoma, the Bible Belt of the USA, there were professors who openly mocked Christianity. After so long, I started to think, "Why do these people hate Christians so much? Are they scared of them? What is going on?". As a young adult, it didn't make sense to me. I just kept passing the classes to get out of school.

However, deep in my heart, I knew there was a god who ruled over everything. I had anti-religious friends. I had friends who were all different kinds of religions. I had enough insight at that time to know I was not able to decide what religion I wanted to follow. The only thing I knew for certain deep down was that I was not an atheist. Honestly, even though I considered some of them friends, they terrified me. I never understood their complete lack of belief in a higher power. I did listen to them in the common areas of school, but that was about it. All of this led me down a windy trail of asking who is right and who is not. What do history and science have to say?

So, like a good researcher, I started reading. I started reading the Bible. I started looking at historical accounts outside of the Bible. I looked at the carbon dating of the Shroud of Turin (Shroud of Jesus of Nazareth), at first I read that it originated from medieval times. However, it came out later that the sample they used for the carbon dating was visibly different from the rest of the shroud and a known patch that had been sewn onto the shroud during the medieval period. They've done numerous scientific studies on the shroud and taken biblical and extra-biblical sources combined to determine that the odds of the shroud belonging to someone other than Jesus of Nazareth are 20 billion to one. They took historical accounts of his wounds and compared them to the images on the shroud, they looked at the decomposition data, pollen samples and more to get to that number. It's truly extraordinary. Some people want the carbon dating to happen again on a different piece. However, every time you carbon-date something that piece is destroyed. I understand why the Catholic Church, the current custodian of the relic, does not want any more of the shroud destroyed.

The historical accounts of Jesus outside of the Bible are valid. The evidence outside of the Bible comes from both Roman and Jewish historians. These non-Christian accounts confirm his execution by Pontius Pilate. They confirmed he was crucified and also the existence of his followers. The historical counts in the Bible are valid as well. The earliest Christian confirmed documentation of Jesus Christ came in 48 to 62 A.D. This came from the apostle Paul's letters. This is the oldest date currently, but I'm sure there will be further breakthroughs in the future.

With everyone screaming, "Where is the proof?" today, I look at 20 billion to one odds and all the historical accounts, biblical and extra-biblical, and I think that is pretty damn much proof Jesus existed. Then people ask where the proof of the miracles is. Many scholars today tell you that these accounts cannot be trusted. Then I say Aristotle, Socrates, and other well-known figures throughout history, who are only known because of historical accounts or texts, cannot be trusted either. You cannot have it both ways.

I have found that most people who argue that Jesus never existed or go after Christians often have very limited knowledge of Christianity. They frequently use the same tactic when discussing things. It is called verse jumping. It is where they will quote several different verses, trying to prove something. They take the verses completely out of context. When you point out what they are doing, they will refuse to read the context of the verse. My advice to Christians in the future is if you're ever discussing with someone who tries to verse jump on you. Make them stay with one verse until you explain that. Their goal is to overwhelm you and get you flustered to the point where you cannot think straight. Do not let them do that. Because once you dive into the text further, their arguments fall apart instantly. They have little to no knowledge of what they heard someone else say. Most people are too lazy to research; therefore, they stumble upon any opposition.

My research led me to the beginning of Christianity. I studied the early Christianity that Jesus of Nazareth started, Catholicism. He made his disciple Peter, the rock upon which he built his foundation. Peter became the first pope. Yes, the disciples passed down some traditions not explicitly mentioned in the Bible. But you have to take into account traditions and beliefs that may not have been directly written in the Bible. 2 Thessalonians 2:15 even says, "So then, brothers and sisters, stand firm and hold fast to the teachings we passed on to you, whether by word of mouth or by letter." (NIV-emphasis added). It took me a while to comprehend this.

Throughout this process, the feeling of emptiness that something was missing in my life started to disappear. I realize now that I was missing that connection with God. I needed that sense of grounding in my life after over 2 years of researching Christianity. I have been fully initiated into the Catholic faith. My family has followed me in making this decision. We enjoy having that sense of working for a bigger picture to help humanity. Yes, we try to help where we can when we can. For me, this is where I needed to be. It feels like home to me. I need the structure that the Catholic faith offers. The reason I did not choose another denomination is that once I looked into the body of evidence, the other denominations were just spinoffs of Catholicism, categorized by what they do not do or do not believe. Are they right? Are they wrong? I don't know. I do hope that everyone ends up in heaven. I know the only way to get to heaven is through Jesus Christ. I hope to help people believe in God the Father, Jesus Christ, and the Holy Spirit.

Through my research of Christianity, I found that the purpose of the church is to worship God. The things I experienced and learned from my childhood interaction with the church that led me away from Christianity were legitimate issues, but my focus was not on the correct thing. My focus was on the people within the church. I found that I was paying too much attention to the individuals within the church and what was going on within the building instead of God. This was my fault for my own ignorance. In my research, I finally got to the point where I was asking questions of several different denominations of Christianity. There was one denomination that never got upset about questions. In the area where I was living at the time, there was a priest named Father Toomey at a Catholic Church. He welcomed any questions. He answered most, if not all, questions right away. He also gave me things to read as well as opposing viewpoints. He himself had been anti-Catholic for a time. He knew how the anti-Catholic crowd thought and what their arguments were before I even needed to ask the questions.

After discussing things with him, I felt more at peace. Yes, he wanted me to join the church, but he also wanted me to have a solid foundation for my faith to grow. He responded when I asked why he was so open with everything and could answer all the questions. He replied, "The Catholic faith has been around for over

2000 years, and we've been scrutinized numerous times. As a faith, we should handle any question with grace." Father Toomey gave me the most genuine sense that he just wanted to save souls that I had ever been around or felt. After speaking with him multiple times and asking my questions, it was easy for me to decide which church I was joining.

After deciding to attend the church that Father Toomey led, I continued to ask questions of him as well as other members of the church. All the members of the church were very welcoming. There was no sense of assigned seats in church. As I continued my questioning, I was introduced to John. He was one of the instructors for the RCIA (Rite of Christian Initiation of Adults) class. He and Father Toomey could see that I wanted a deeper understanding of the Catholic faith from active members. They both suggested that I enroll in the RCIA class. This was so I could get a better understanding of what the church actually taught and believed. They also made it very clear that I would not be pressured into becoming Catholic; they were just happy someone was interested in learning about their faith. After some deep reflection, I enrolled in RCIA classes.

During the RCIA classes, I did everything you would expect a physician or someone who didn't understand the Catholic faith to do; I questioned many things. To my surprise, they did not get aggravated at my questions. John became a big part of answering those questions, both in class and at personal meetings. Growing up, I saw most, if not all, Christian men as pacifists; so, focused on turning the other cheek that they forgot to stand up for themselves or their faith. They seemed to be willing to cater to everyone's immorality and were more worried about offending people than saving souls. This was a big sticking point for me. I knew God was real and believed that Jesus came to save us but I could not reconcile being a man and protector with being so submissive to a corrupt world. One of the things that John told me that will stick with me forever was that "Jesus was not just nice". Yes, Jesus wants to bring everyone to God through him. However, Jesus was not afraid to show his strength and teach them to sin no more. We talked about the example of the adulteress who was about to be stoned. Jesus saved her by telling the people, he who has not sinned shall cast the first stone. They all dropped their stones and walked away. Then Jesus looked at the woman and told her to sin no more. His purpose is to redeem souls and show us the correct path- save yes, but also to not tolerate continued sinful behavior. I believe this was the missing piece for me. Being a father myself, I need to be able to protect my family physically and spiritually. Once I found out that I could be a Christian and still have the ability to defend my family and faith, I was relieved. I continued RCIA classes and learned the structure of the church and family. I learned about the reason Mass is held the same way every time. For me, the structure of Mass is very soothing. I need stability in my life.

Since joining the Catholic faith, I have attended Mass at least weekly. The Eucharistic celebration is a fantastic thing to witness. If you have never been to a Catholic Mass, I strongly encourage you to go at least once. Don't worry about the standing up or kneeling aspect of the Mass; take it in. Everything about mass is to bring you closer to Jesus. It is to celebrate Jesus's sacrifice for us. There is no loud band or loud music. There's no yelling during a church sermon as you focus on God and the sacrifice of Jesus Christ. It is truly a beautiful thing to see and experience.

Since finding God, I have been more productive and goal-oriented than ever. My wife has been super supportive. She helps me in so many ways, it's unbelievable. When a husband and wife become one and are goal-oriented, nothing can stand in their way, especially if they are doing it for the benefit of Christ. I believe that my practice is for the Father Almighty. My goal is to help spread the word. I will do my best to heal all people, including anyone who wants to be treated like a whole person and have an actual physician-patient relationship. I encourage you to look at Ascent Healthcare in Maryville, Tennessee, to see if we can help you achieve your health goals.

God has placed this idea in my brain for the last several years. I have lived the corporate medicine lifestyle. I have felt like I was beating my head into a wall daily. I have fought with the administration to be able to treat patients appropriately. I was always told that it is not in the budget or that there is insufficient money by the administration. Somehow, they are always able to find more administrative positions and increases in salary for administrators. Yet, physicians and other providers and staff who are actually the ones delivering care and service are treated like numbers and advised that we are expendable. These are just a few examples that have led me to break away from the corporate side. I will not tell you that I was not scared in this decision. Whenever I started to get scared, God would place someone or something in front of me to keep me motivated to keep moving forward.

I believe God was instrumental in my starting my own clinic. My frustrations with corporate medicine led me to this epiphany: I do not fit the corporate model. This transition occurred at the same time as my becoming fully initiated into the Catholic church. In medicine, you have to have some belief in a higher calling. Mine has transformed me into a physician who ensures I can treat the whole person: mind, body, and spirit. You can do well in two of these areas, but you're not at optimal health if one is off.

We are all spiritual beings. At this point, it is obvious that I believe in the Blessed Trinity and the spirit of Catholicism. I hope to bring souls to Christ. However, I know that not everyone will share my Catholic Faith. That is okay. Regardless of what spiritual path someone follows, I want them to acknowledge and address it to reach their highest health potential.

These are going to be the things that I will be helping patients with moving forward. By doing this, I will ensure everyone is at maximal health and that all three areas—mind, body, and spirit—are addressed. Yes, these words originated from A.T. Still (the founder of Osteopathic Medicine). However, as physicians, sometimes we get too focused on the body and forget the other two. I'm aiming to correct this in my practice. This is what God has led me to do. That way, I can treat people with a better understanding of the whole person.

I hope you, the reader, take from this chapter that you do not have to go with an authority figure's opinions. Everyone can have their own opinions and beliefs, and you should challenge them to see if they stand or crumble. That being said, you should also not use your position of authority to push that opinion down subordinates' throats. One should be willing to research to come to their own conclusions. You should be able to ask multiple resources. Don't just make your decisions based on one source. Lastly, know what is in your heart. If you feel emptiness, try figuring out what that means to you. My disconnect was between God, Jesus Christ, and the Holy Spirit. Once I got this back, I was much more at peace. Even when I was starting the business and had no income coming in, I was still much more peaceful than I ever had been before Christ. I hope everyone can find this peace in their life.

Life Lessons

1. Do not blindly trust authority figures like teachers or college professors.
2. Do your research, know the facts, and find what is essential to you.
3. Be willing to be uncomfortable in your searching for the truth.

Questions for the Reader

1. When was the last time you questioned something you were told?

   _____

   _____

2. When is the last time you studied your beliefs?

   _____

   _____

3. What's a main takeaway from this chapter?

   _____

   _____

Chapter 11

Fight For Your Health

Once I made it out of residency, I remember feeling fatigued, dragging myself to work, being moody, and lacking ambition. I had minimal energy to do the things that I enjoyed. Fishing and hunting were becoming much more of a hassle. Hell, just walking to my deer stand, I would get winded. But most importantly, rolling on the floor with the kids, I would get short-winded quickly. I realized this is what happens whenever you focus on too many "other" things mixed with chronic stress. Your cortisol levels are elevated, causing you to gain weight. I was not working out like I should've been. I would go to the gym maybe once or twice a week, or for a walk. I remember thinking to myself, this is not who I want to be. I was considered obese by the BMI chart. But after looking at body composition, I was 30 pounds overweight.

I didn't want to watch my children from the sidelines. I wanted to be active in their lives. All fathers say that they will die for their children. One day, the question came to me, "But would you live for your children?" This hit me hard. I started taking my health more seriously. I've always been serious about my health-taking care of my diabetes, etc.; however, I took it to the next level. I started doing programs to help keep me active longer in life. I also started taking my nutrition seriously. I'm knocking on that 40-year-old mark. I want to keep going like I am now for at least another 30-35 years. My family deserves the best I can give them. Therefore, I have to put in the effort every day. I cannot be the typical 30 to 40-year-old American male who is overweight and barely moves. I have to be better than that. My family deserves better than that. I want to be the father who lives for his wife and children.

I will be the dad who wrestles with them on the floor. I'll be the dad who trains with them in our weight room. I will be the dad who runs with them in the yard. The dad who carries them up the stairs for as long as I can. I know these precious memories will soon end. Don't get me wrong. I enjoy sitting in my rocking chair and snuggling with the children while watching a show. However, I get much more enjoyment out of playing with them. Having water or Nerf gun wars is far more enjoyable for everyone involved. It is always fun to hear that the children first want to wrestle on the floor when I return from a trip. They also want to show me their new skills from ju-jitsu. They love making Dad fall and making me tap out. It brings them and me so much joy. I didn't always realize these were the moments that I did all the extra work for, but I am damn glad I did it. We try to keep the kids as active as possible. This keeps their imaginations and physical activity very high. We very rarely use TV. Occasionally, I will watch a hockey game, Dr Oakley, the original Lord of the Rings trilogy (my wife's influence- I told you she is a nerd), or something like that. Otherwise, we play chess, Battleships, or some physical activity that will grow their minds.

For my wife, I want to be the man who can do what makes her feel loved. I want to be able to fix things and move the furniture around whenever she has an impulse to change things. I want her to see that I'm also investing in our long-term future by investing in my health. This investment in my health led me to look into potential cures for my diabetes, finally. My wife and I started looking and found a trial that was going on in the USA. This trial was in Chicago. My wife sent the initial email for me. I had waited a week after finding the trial to reach out to them. I was so used to being diabetic. I was not sure what anything else would be like. I was 11 years old when I was diagnosed. It is hard for me to remember a time when I was not diabetic. I think being non-diabetic scared me. So, my wife got the ball rolling and sent that introduction email when I was ready. The next day, I received a call from Dr. Witkowski, the primary investigator in the trial. After discussing the trial with Dr. Witkowski, a board-certified transplant surgeon, he explained the procedure of placing islet-cell stem cells into my liver. This is to supply enough blood for the islet cells to mature. Once the stem cells mature, they start producing insulin and glucagon as they should. I would have to be on immunosuppressive medication for the rest of my life.

The first step in the trial was to do initial bloodwork to confirm that the trial met the criteria. I also needed a physical exam from Dr. Witkowski. This is routine for any patient. I was fine with it. I also had to do other tests since this is a trial study to ensure I was in optimal health and to track over the long term to ensure the cells and the medication aren't causing any harm. I had to do cardiac clearance, including an echocardiogram, an EKG, and a treadmill stress test, as well as a four-hour glucose tolerance test. The glucose tolerance test made me feel like crap since my blood sugar went so high. After all the initial testing and procedures, the next step was to see if I qualified for the islet cell transplant trial.

I soon found out that I qualified to be in the trial. It was almost like a weight was lifted off my shoulders. They originally scheduled me a month out to receive my transplant. Everything was set up for me to come in and get the transplant. I got admitted to the hospital for the procedure, just before receiving the first round of medications to start immunosuppression, I received a phone call shortly before midnight. It was Dr. Witkowski reporting that I would not be getting a transplant. The cells did not pass the final tests. I was devastated. It was like a gut punch sitting there in the hospital bed. I had been waiting for six months since starting the initial test to receive this transplant, and now, at the last minute, it was being pulled away. Dr. Witkowski explained that they do multiple tests just before transplant, and one of the tests, the stem cell islet-cells, did not pass. He did not want to take a chance on giving me cells that were not going to be effective. As a physician, I understood this completely. However, as a patient, it was a gut-wrenching experience. I tried to stay positive. This did not mean I was out of the trial. It just meant that I would be delayed in getting my islet cells.

After returning home from the failed attempt, I was down for a bit. I chose to look at this as just a trial run to make sure we had everything ready. Then, within a couple of days, they advised me that they had another batch of cells and would be flying me back to Chicago in three days for a transplant. At that moment, I was excited but also a bit apprehensive. Was it going to be like the last time I got there, go through the whole admission process, and then have the rug pulled out from under me again? But then I thought back to the rest of my life. Most things in my life require a few attempts before things go as planned. I just laughed in my head and maybe out loud. I had faith that it was going to happen this time.

During the lead-up to the procedure, I also had to juggle work and home life. It is hard to schedule and reschedule patients when the timeline keeps changing. My office manager was amazing during this process. She knew how important this was to me. She advised me multiple times, tell me what you need, and we'll make it happen. I honestly felt guilty for leaving my colleagues to pick up the slack from me. Although I knew the bigger picture, this would make me a better father, husband, and physician in the long run.

Now back in Chicago for the second attempt at transplant, I started by myself in a hospital bed. I was anxiously waiting, watching the clock before I was scheduled to get my medicine to start my immunosuppression. I was expecting another phone call from Dr. Witkowski telling me the islet cells did not pass the tests again. I received a phone call from Dr. Witkowski, but he was very upbeat and excited this time. He said, "We have the islet cells, and they passed all the tests". Then he asked me, "Are you ready to start your immunosuppression"? I paused. I knew this procedure had the potential to cure me. However, there was a slight hesitation. I would be leaving the life that I was comfortable with. Then I realized that to get to the new life I wanted, my old life would have to die. Dr. Witkowski gave me a few moments before he politely asked again. "Are you ready to start immunosuppression? " I said, "Hell yes!! Let's do this!!"

A few moments after I had spoken with Dr. Witkowski, the nurse walked in and asked, "Are you ready to start?" I told them yes; I was ready to start the next leg of my journey. They began by giving me thymoglobulin plus a whole cocktail of other medications. I am unable to give the complete specifics of the medication that I was given since this is still in trial.

As the medication went into my IV, I lay there and thought about what my life could be like without having to take insulin all the time. Without having to ensure I kept my insulin from getting too warm or cold. I could finally take my family on extended hikes, versus the 2–3-hour hikes that we currently did. We could do overnight camping trips in the woods. We could travel without making sure hotels had fridges or traveling with ice chests all the time for me to put my insulin in. I didn't realize how conditioned I was to deal with diabetes until I lay there in the hospital bed thinking of what I would do if I didn't have to take insulin. It was great to sit there and daydream about all the possibilities. I contemplated calling a recruiter to see if I could join the military now. I would be a 36-year-old recruit. As a physician, I could enlist much older than most people. I honestly did not know what to do with my new freedom if this worked.

I felt pretty well when I woke up the next morning, lying in a hospital bed. As you would expect, I was pretty sore from the hospital bed. No matter what hospital you're in, these things are uncomfortable as hell. My wife came in that morning. Due to a patient scheduling conflict, she had to come in the day after me. I was happy when she got there. I was less bored sitting in the hospital room. The thymoglobulin that they were giving me was starting to take effect. I was feeling run down. I was also beginning to develop body aches. They said these were typical side effects. So, I didn't think much about it. I just kept thinking about the daydream I had the night before and the endless possibilities. I had two days of thymoglobulin before I was able to undergo the transplant.

During the second day, while being hospitalized, the medications continued, and I was still having the same side effects of muscle aches and fatigue. However, I kept walking in the hallways multiple times a day. My wife and I started to discuss things such as the business we had been contemplating opening. We kept putting a hold on that. There was always something in the way, some next step we had to take before we could get there. We both were hesitant because it was an uncertain option. We knew the things we wanted to do differently in our lives. We knew owning our own business would be better in the long run. However, we, probably mostly me, were scared deep down of failure. Then I got to thinking, I've seen many people who have started businesses and who are successful. I am just as smart as they are. If I can get over the fear and undergo a transplant, why in the hell can I not start a business? I realized it was my problem. I was the barrier. I decided then and there that if I were successful with this transplant, I would start a business that would be able to change the face of medicine. My wife laughed and said, "We're making this decision now while in the hospital?" I said, "Yes, why not now? We're discussing planning our future and what we want to do". So, on the day of the transplant, June 17, 2024, we decided that we would make our own path and push for what we wanted in life.

Shortly after my discussion with my wife, I was then moved to the ICU since they were starting me on an insulin drip. The insulin drip had to be started before the transplant. Then I was going to be moved to the procedure room and have the islet-cell transplanted. Again, since this procedure is still in trial, I cannot go into the specifics of the procedure. As I was wheeled off to the procedure room, I was nervous. Dr. Witkowski actually helped push the hospital bed to the procedure room. He was calm and upbeat about the procedure as well as excited. This put me at ease. I knew that he would take care of me once I was in the procedure room. Dr. Witkowski is a classic old-school doctor. When you're under his care, he takes care of everything. Once I got to the procedure room,

Dr. Witkowski asked me again. "Are you ready?". This time, I didn't hesitate; I said yes.

I remember waking up back in the ICU, and my wife was with me. As I came to, I asked her how the procedure went. She told me they said everything went well as far as she knew. I was relieved. Then, out of the blue, I realized how sore I was. They gave me some Tylenol for pain. The Tylenol worked initially for the pain, but after a couple of hours, the Tylenol was not as effective anymore. My muscles and fatigue had gotten much worse. I also noticed that despite the amount of fluids I was getting, my urine production had decreased substantially. It was difficult to urinate. I was still in the ICU, so they decided to give me some stronger pain medication to see if that would help. Being a very opioid naïve person, what they gave me should've knocked out any pain that I was having. However, it did not; things seemed to get worse.

I started to have issues catching my breath. I also spiked a temperature. I was burning up. Or at least it felt as though I was burning up. I still could not urinate. I ended up getting a Foley catheter placed after they scanned my bladder and realized I was not able to urinate and had a completely full bladder. That damn sure was not fun. I also became nauseous and started vomiting. They immediately took me in for a CT scan. There was nothing conclusive on CT, only a small amount of blood within the abdomen which is to be expected after the transplant. With no clear source, they treated my symptoms. I was given anti-nausea medication, and they continue to increase my pain medicine. They gave me Tylenol and icepacks for my fever. Even with the medicine and multiple icepacks they couldn't get my temperature under 102. This continued all night.

My wife has informed me of much of the story overnight. I do not remember of it. I do remember vomiting a few more times and getting an NG (nasogastric) tube placed. An NG tube is a flexible plastic tube that goes in your nose, down your throat, and into your stomach to help keep you from vomiting. It sucks out the gastric contents from your stomach. I believe I'll take a couple of Foleys over an NG tube any day. I have a deeper appreciation for patients who have had to get an NG tube now. The next morning, there was not much change in my condition, except now they had me on a PCA pain pump. I was able to dose myself with medication every 15 minutes. I was trying to hit it before my fifteen minutes though. I was doing this to breathe. Without the pain medication, I could not breathe. Even with it, I was gasping, but it was much worse without it. I had only used one opioid pill in my life before this hospitalization. That was when my wisdom teeth were cut out. I received a prescription from the dentist for hydrocodone 5 mg tablets. I took one and vomited immediately. I dumped those down the toilet and never retook another opioid. But now in the hospital, I was requiring them to breathe and maintain some sense of calm. I was going in and out of consciousness, and I knew something was terribly wrong. I didn't know what yet.

With me continuing to deteriorate, I started getting more worried. Dr. Witkowski was gone; he had to attend a conference to present on the trial. The fellow who was supervising my care in the hospital during the day did not seem to care about what was going wrong with me. His questioning made me realize that he thought I was a druggy and withdrawing. He kept asking what I usually took outside the hospital and telling my wife that there was no way I should be needing or able to tolerate that much narcotic. The more she tried to explain that something wasn't right, the more aggressively he dismissed her concerns. She was worried, as a physician herself (with a much clearer brain than I had just then), she knew something was very wrong, but the fellow had already made up his mind and would not listen to her or me. I could see she was getting agitated. I asked her to let it go; I needed her to be there with me, and I didn't want them to kick her out. I was getting more and more concerned by the hour. Especially now that I knew Dr. Walkowski was not taking care of me and the fellow didn't want to look into the problem. We did not want to deal with the fellow during the day since his solution was to decrease the pain meds and increase the ice. The nursing staff was excellent throughout the day, but the fellow hamstrung them. Later in the evening, the night team came on. My nurse was amazing and immediately decided to do something before my wife or I said a word. Just like being a resident, a good nurse can save your ass as a patient. She called the nurse practitioner who was on that night and strongly advised her to see me. When the Nurse Practitioner showed up, I was laying in the hospital bed with six different ice packs on my chest and abdomen as well as a bag of ice between my legs and under my arms.

That Nurse Practitioner listened to my symptoms, concerns, and the timeline. My wife had practically begged the fellow to hear her earlier in the day. We didn't have to ask the NP; she walked in listening and looking for a source. After a bullet point history and quick exam, she decided that I had probably developed serum sickness. She had seen it a few times prior, although I seemed to be having a very strong reaction and a little quicker than usual. Earlier in the day, the fellow had dismissed serum sickness as a possibility. He said that only my skeletal muscles should be affected and not affect my breathing. We tried to remind him that the diaphragm is a skeletal muscle, but he disagreed. The Nurse Practitioner didn't seem to have a problem with my presentation; she started me on IV steroids immediately. Within 30 minutes of receiving the first dose of steroids, my pain was gone, and I was able to breathe.

The next day, when the attendings showed up with the fellow, I informed the attending that the fellow could wait in the hallway. After receiving the steroids the night before, my body was doing much better. I was still sore and fatigued, but I could now think clearly, my temperature had decreased considerably, and I could breathe. The attending advised me that, yes, I most likely had serum sickness. He explained to me that thymoglobulin had caused me to develop serum sickness because I had consumed rabbits as a child. This caused my body to have a very aggressive immune response to the medication. The medicine was trying to kill my immune system while the immune system was trying to kill the medicine, so it was a double attack at the same time within my body. My body's response was to start shutting down. Therefore, they had to give me high-dose steroids every six hours. From the time I started the steroids, I did not require any more opioid pain medication. I went back to just Tylenol. I also advised the attending that I did not want to see the fellow. The attending understood and gave me his cell phone number. He also apologized for taking them so long to determine what was happening. I do not blame the fellow for not getting the diagnosis right. I blame the fellow for his poor bedside manner, egotistical attitude, condescension, and, most importantly, disrespect toward my wife. This is what led me to dismiss him from taking care of me.

The next few days, I started to regain my strength. I was back walking in the hallways. I finally left the transplant unit (but not the hospital) for decent food. Being on the steroids meant I was having to burn through insulin like crazy. The islet cells I had just been transplanted with had not matured. This meant they were producing very little insulin. Once we started the correct treatment for my serum sickness, it was a great feeling. When they informed me that I began to produce insulin the next morning, I was amazed. My body had not produced insulin since I was 11 years old. That was very exciting. Each day, I would go further down the hallway to push myself. I would do a few additional workouts in the room. My wife had now been out of work for over a week and had had to push back her return date because of my delayed recovery with the serum sickness; she was also missing our two children. But she did not want to leave me alone, so she called my father to take over. My father showed up and took over care of me now that I was stable.

This was not his or my first time staying in the hospital for a long time. He was there for all my hospitalizations when I was a child. He came in and was supportive the whole time. He was concerned about the amount of weight I had lost. That's what happens when you don't eat for three days and your body is burning energy trying to set itself on fire. I ended up losing almost 25 pounds in three days. The other thing that concerned him was how emotional I was. I usually don't cry in front of people, even with fear, pain, and lack of control in my situation during the hospitalization, I controlled my outward emotions. Until the steroids hit me, some people get agitated and angry on steroids. I, on the other hand, cried for absolutely no reason. I felt bad for not keeping this stuff inside. In my family, we pick on each other constantly; it is how we show our love to each other. They knew this was out of character for me. My dad and wife never said a word about it. I am grateful for the steroids. They are what stabilized me and got me on the right track. But they did make my eyes very leaky.

Since I was feeling better and eating again, we could relax a little bit. We started watching the Stanley Cup playoffs, where the Florida Panthers played the Edmonton Oilers. Of course, we were going for the Florida Panthers. I had started to watch hockey more and more over the last 10 years. My father still didn't understand hockey. So, I got to educate him on the rules while we were in the hospital room. It was game seven of the cup finals. Dr. Witkowski was back from his conference. He came into the room to check on me. He looked up at the TV and said, "Oh crap, the games are on!". He made sure I was doing well. Then said that he wanted to go home and watch the game, and if anything changed, to call him. I don't blame him for leaving the hospital to watch the Final hockey game of the year. I'm sure it's much more enjoyable watching the game at his house than in the hospital room. Again, the beds and furniture in hospital rooms are very uncomfortable.

Things were on the downhill slide. I was getting better day by day. They eventually let me leave the hospital. However, I had to stay in Chicago for another two weeks after discharge. Dad and I are basically playing around Chicago. It was a fun time. I saw some things in Chicago that I probably would never have done. Typically, on all my trips, I go to a conference or something like that. I characteristically do not do many touristy things. Being a country kid, I still do not like crowds. Chicago is one big crowd. So there my dad and I are, two Okies in Chicago, trying to figure out where to go and what to do in this big city. Dad is far more used to cows than people. So, we ended up watching many people from the hotel lobby. We made friends with the hotel staff. One of the hotel staff members would tell us stories about people who had come through and would watch with us. Many times, we would sit at the table and shake our heads as an individual who was definitely challenging some type of social norm would walk by. Sometimes my father and/or Dwight, the hotel staffer, would go. "What the hell is that?" or "What the hell are they trying to do?" It was pretty entertaining to say the least. We spent a lot of time in Hyde Park. If you're ever in Chicago, it seems to be separated by parks. It was nice being within walking distance of anything you wanted. The only problem was that I was still healing from the transplant, so walking too far was out of the question.

Finally, after the two weeks, I went in for a checkup with Dr. Witkowski, who gave me the green light to return home. We arranged air travel back home once he gave me the okay to go home. My dad and I parted ways at the airport as he was going back to Oklahoma, and I was going back to northern Pennsylvania, where I lived at the time. It was nice spending that amount of time with my father. He is definitely the man who's always been in my corner. It is great to have someone in your corner who wants you to be better than they are. However, with my father, those are big shoes to fill. He's always loved his family. He's always put his kids first. Even during the times when he wanted to leave my mother when we were young, he did not. He stayed and was our protector. He did the best he could with the cards he was dealt.

Once I made it back home, things continued to improve. I was still on some steroids; however, we were tapering off of them. The first few days off the taper were tolerable, then I started to get pain in my arms and legs again. I thought it was just me being tired. I didn't want to admit I was getting sick again. I kept these feelings under wraps as my wife was still horrified by the hospitalization. However, I cannot hide much from her. She realized I was doing less and less each day and that I was sleeping more. She called Dr. Witkowski, and he advised me to start back on the steroids. As soon as I did, the symptoms went away. Thymoglobulin will last in your system for three months. My body hated that medication, and it hated me. The feelings were mutual. I am glad that I will never have to take that medication again. So, after another week of steroids, we tapered off again. This time, enough of the medication was out of my system so that I did not go back into serum sickness.

I was very thankful for the serum sickness being gone. When I returned from Chicago, my children had to stay with their grandparents as they had both caught a virus. With me being severely immunosuppressed, they had to stay away. When my children returned home, we could not do the usual wrestling around like we had before. It is almost like they treated me as if I were something breakable, and the medications and transplant had taken some of my strength. I knew it would take time. But they were happy to just lean and snuggle on me now that I was back. I missed them, too.

Little by little, day by day, we got back to our usual selves. We started wrestling again. After a couple of months, I was beginning to feel strong enough to start jiu-jitsu again. I did receive the clearance from the doctor before going. Once on the jiu-jitsu mat, I realized I was still a long way from returning to my usual self. I could only roll for maybe 30 seconds before I was winded completely. I am not talking about winded breathing hard. No! I'm talking about huffing and puffing, trying to catch your breath, and it feels like your body is just absolutely drained, and it's hard to move. I made it through three rotations before I had to call quits. Then I realized that because I was so winded, I was putting more pressure on my knees and the top of my left foot than I was used to. They had been scratched up. Typically, this would not have concerned me except now I was on immunosuppressive medication. We doctored them the best we could, but they got infected anyway. After a few rounds of oral antibiotics, I had to go back into the hospital to get IV antibiotics. This meant more time away from my family back in Chicago. I was glad that I was able to go back to Chicago and get the necessary treatment, although this just showed me that I needed to take my time with healing. I needed to stop rushing the process. I had to realize that I am not bulletproof anymore. Admitting this to myself was very difficult. I had always been able to use sheer will to get through just about anything. I had to get used to my body and its new healing ability.

After the incident with my foot and knee infection, I decided to put jiu-jitsu on hold for a while. I just focused on healing both my body and my mind. I was still doing my exercises in the morning before work. I like picking up heavy things and moving them from one place to another. So, I would do this workout and some workouts in the evenings occasionally. I knew this would help my body fight against insulin resistance and make it so that I didn't need as much insulin in the long term.

After continuing to stay active and taking all the medication the way I was supposed to, I was able to come totally off all insulin at the end of January 2025. This was a little over six months after my transplant. I finally had the freedom of not being hooked up to an insulin pump. It was a weird feeling. For many months after I stopped using an insulin pump, I would wake up in the middle of the night, reaching for my pump to move it with me whenever I rolled over. My body was used to taking that thing with me wherever I went.

My family and I enjoyed our newfound freedom for a couple of months. Our first trip was to Gettysburg, PA, where we walked to the battlefield without having to keep my pump out of the sun. It was liberating. Then we noticed my son started acting sick. He was sluggish, like he was fighting off a virus. This lasted for a few days. Then we noticed he was sleeping more and drinking more as well. I did a finger-stick to check his blood sugar, which was over 300, three times normal. Throughout the whole process of the trial, I was doing it for a better future for type 1 diabetics. Yes, it was a potential cure for me, but it was also a step towards hope and a future for others like me. I knew there was a chance one or both of my children could become diabetic. However, it was a low chance. It was just slightly higher than the average person. I was taking my son to the children's emergency room, over an hour from our house. This was probably one of the hardest drives I will ever have to make. On the way down, he held my wife's hand because he was scared and asked when he could have "daddy's surgery" so he didn't have to be diabetic. I was astonished that a four-year-old child would have that amount of awareness of his situation. The whole way down, I kept blaming myself.

We finally made it to the hospital. I opened his door, took him out of his car seat, and, while my wife was getting the other stuff to go into the hospital, I told him a lot of things were going to happen in the hospital, and he probably wasn't going to like any of them. He asked me if things would hurt, and I told him, "Yes, but the nurses and doctors are doing things just to make you better, Bud". He said OKAY. I also told him he'd done nothing wrong. That he would have to live like Daddy did before the surgery. I hugged him and told him, "I love you, little buddy". He hugged me and said, "Love you, Daddy". In that moment, my heart was torn inside my chest. I never let him see that it was eating me alive, watching him have to go through this. I smiled at him and told him he would be okay. Mommy and Daddy were with him, and we were not leaving his side. Then I carried him into the hospital.

In the emergency room, my boy did very well. He allowed the team to take care of him. He would ask questions and flirt with his nurse. He even held still when they did the IV. We had a hold of him just in case, but he didn't need it. He cried for just a few seconds, then it was done. The only thing that kept making him cry was the finger-sticks. It was a quick process getting through the ED to a room. I called ahead on the way down and spoke to the on-call doctor; they knew we were coming and why, so they were expecting his results and quickly moved us through the ER. Sometimes being a doctor means learning how to work within the system and using it to your advantage. Once my wife and I knew that our son was okay and being treated, we could breathe a sigh of relief. While he was asleep, we both had moments of letting go of our emotions. We knew that life was going to be different for us now. Luckily, we had already made life changes that set us up to care for him. My wife had already quit working to be at home with the kids.

After the second day of being in the hospital, the crying with the finger sticks went away, and he was doing well with his shots. With him being four and not having good dexterity with his hands and fingers yet, it was up to me and his mom to give him the insulin shots. With me being a former diabetic as well as a physician and my wife being a physician, we were able to go home after just over 48 hours. My son was fortunate that we caught it very early. He did not go into DKA (Diabetic Keto Acidosis). My son has done very well with his diabetes. He still continues to this day to do better than the majority of insulin-requiring adults with diabetes. He does very well in most situations if you tell him the truth beforehand. I had several nurses during his hospitalization who would look at me like I was crazy when I told them things were going to hurt. Then he did well with them. He expected the needle sticks in the finger stick to hurt; he wasn't surprised. He needed someone to tell him the truth. I would much rather have him know the truth and be able to trust me in tough times. I will not lose that trust. After he did well, the nurses realized the benefits of being honest with a child who is already scared. They are more resilient than we give them credit for.

Once my son was home, we returned to normal as much as possible. His big sister is very conscientious about what he eats, and so is he. She is basically a little mommy figure at the age of 6 years old. And I thought she mothered him before! I am fortunate to have my wife and our daughter, who help care for him. My wife wakes up instantly if his monitor goes off in the middle of the night. I pick on her occasionally that she did not get up when my monitor went off. She laughs and just tells me it's because he is her baby. I am perfectly okay with this. He is her baby as well as my baby.

People asked me if going through the trial was worth it. They say, We see that you went through a lot. I agree, I went through a lot that the transplant team and I were not anticipating. The majority of people who go through trials and transplants will not have the challenges I did. I am happy I went through the study. I am glad I'm continuing to go through the study. I continue to give them information multiple times a week. The study will help numerous type 1 diabetics in the future. If I could better the research for them and now my son, it would be well worth it. Yes, I am still off insulin. It is a great thing to be off insulin. I'm not constantly fighting to keep my blood sugar at a normal level. I don't have to carry snacks with me for myself anymore. Now I take them for my son, because just playing outside or wrestling can make his blood sugar drop very low. We have to account for everything for him, just like we did with me. So yes, absolutely, I am glad I did this study. I would do it again. Even knowing that I would go through the serum sickness, thoughts that I may die, and all the other challenges during the hospitalization. The answer is without a doubt, HELL YES, I would do it again. Because now they know what to expect. The transplant teams can plan better. They can prevent these complications in future patients, and one may even be my son.

Life Lessons

1. Be willing to take a chance at improving yourself. Focus on your health; without health, you have nothing.
2. Be disciplined in your diet and exercise.
3. Never doubt the importance of family motivation. Please make it a family goal to be healthier.

Questions for the Reader

1. Do you schedule time for meals and exercise?

   _____

   _____

2. Do you make plans that require some fitness? If not, start today.

   _____

   _____

3. Do you discuss plans to become healthy with your doctor? If not, make that a priority at your next appointment.

   _____

   _____

4. What's the main takeaway from this chapter?

   _____

   _____

Chapter 12
Divine Intervention

It is funny how the right people appear at the correct time and place. I have had numerous times when I thought I was done. I could go no further in life. It was time to settle down and stop dreaming. Then BAM, something or someone shows up out of nowhere to challenge my thinking. One of the first people to directly challenge me was Dr. Solitario after I was diagnosed with type 1 diabetes at 11 years old. She challenged me to go to school and learn a trade. She wanted me to use my brain instead of my muscles. I told her I didn't like school, that she was crazy suggesting that I should go to college. She looked at me straight in the eyes and said, "Get over yourself, stop feeling sorry for yourself. You are going to go to college, and you will do something great. You will help people".

I had never previously thought about college after high school. I actually did not like going to school. I wanted to go and be a Navy SEAL. Now that was out the window because of this damn disease. After I was diagnosed with diabetes, I figured I would either work in the oil field or work at Goodyear like my father. Nothing else really crossed my mind. Over the years, Doc got me thinking more and more about going to college. She never gave up. Every other visit, she would question what I was doing in school and how my college plans were going. This lady was very damn persistent; I will give her that. She would laugh when I told her I was not attending college.

Once I was in college, I was doing very well in pre-nursing classes to become a flight medic. Yes, I wanted the adrenaline rushes from flying in a chopper and helping people. Some things never change. The professor of my microbiology class challenged me to take the MCAT for medical school. I actually asked him if he had a screw or two loose in his head. He laughed and said, "You have the personality of someone who would make a good doctor. I have seen you interact with other students and help teach them. You can deal with difficult concepts. You always do well on my test. Also, your humor will put people at ease". He asked, "Have you ever thought of being a physician?". I was dumbfounded. I didn't know what to say other than "no, I never gave it a thought". His reply was, "Just think it over and see if that's something you want to do. The next MCAT will be in one month. You should take that test". It was shocking that a professor would encourage me to be a physician. Also, he had looked up when the next MCAT in the area would be. The thought of being a physician had never crossed my mind previously. Growing up as the guy who was labeled the so-called dumb kid in class in elementary school because I could not read in grade school, this seemed like a fantasy. I was very intrigued by the challenge from my professor. He knew the best way to get me to do anything was to challenge me. When I am challenged, I seem to do my best work. I want to tell you that I did fantastically on that MCAT and got into medical school on one try. But you already read the story about how the standardized tests kicked my butt, and it took me learning to read again. Then I was able to conquer that damn test.

A few days before I agreed to take help from my soon-to-be in-laws I was having a difficult day in college. It wasn't just school that was causing issues. There was family drama as well. It seemed during my undergraduate years my parents were fighting constantly, and my mother would continue to reach out for advice and support. Yes, I knew she was messing up her own life. I didn't know how to set up boundaries at that time. I struggled with keeping up with the schoolwork, preparing for the next MCAT, and dealing with the family stuff. I was at a breaking point. So, I went for a walk.

I didn't usually walk the way that I did that day. I ended up close to a bus stop. I decided to sit at this bus stop, rest, and think for a few minutes. A stranger sat down next to me and noticed I was in a daze after reaching the end of my bandwidth from dealing with family stuff and school. They just sat next to me and asked how things were going. Without thinking or saying the typical lie of "I'm fine". The words "I am done with all this bullshit" came out. He looked at me and smiled. He was a 40-50-year-old black gentleman. By his appearance, he had had a rough life. He said, "I understand that. What keeps me going is knowing that this too shall pass and that tomorrow is another day filled with potential. It is up to us to decide if that is good or bad". That is the first and only time I ever saw that gentleman. Those words calmed me down, and I could escape the downward spiral I had found myself in. Occasionally, I think of that moment and wonder if that was the moment my path was set in stone. The random act of kindness from a stranger helped me greatly; it kept me from walking away from college entirely. I was reminded by that interaction that my outlook on life is up to me. I needed to stop letting external things dictate my emotions or my mood.

After that meeting with my microbiology professor, I thought long and hard about my options. I was already an EMT and had been working as one for several years. I started to watch things differently when dropping off patients in the Emergency Room. I focused more attention on what the physicians were doing. The more I watched, the more I realized I wanted to be a physician. I switched my major from pre-nursing to premed. Since I was already two years into college, this put me back into some sophomore-level classes as a junior in college. I met more science professors by switching majors and met more hardcore science nerds. By this time, I was the president of the biology club. This is how I met my wife for the first time. I would love to tell you it was love at first sight. However, per her, it was the third time we met. But this was the first time I laid down memory. I remember sitting next to her in class, just wanting to speak to her. So, I sat on her desk. I gave her the choice of talking to me, ignoring me, or, probably, the more comical version, pushing me off her desk and onto the floor. She chose to speak to me. Thank God!!

Meeting my wife in college has been the best thing that could have happened to me. After tricking her into our first date by pretending I didn't understand the concepts on our zoology homework and asking for help (of course, she agreed to help since she was a nice person and one of the biggest nerds I have ever met), we got to know each other. Her original plan was to leave Cameron University College after the following two semesters and transfer to the more prestigious Oklahoma University with a medical school. She was not in the mindset of making friends or connections. So, this was a challenge for me. The more we talked, the more we had in common with our plans. We realize that we were both on the premed route. She had always wanted to be a physician. As always, I took the more indirect path. It is just not my style to do things the easiest way possible.

We became study partners and friends first. From the beginning of our relationship, I always annoyed my wife with how well I could do, especially in lab situations where it was more hands-on. The classroom exam portion is where she excelled the most. She could never make an A in the lab portion, which frustrated her greatly. Once we started studying together, this changed. I taught her the secret to getting through any science lab and doing well. She was completely dumbfounded about how I was able to do this. Because at that time, I was working three different jobs. I worked as an EMT and fitness instructor at the campus gym, and I continued farm work. I would show up to class extremely tired and sleep occasionally during the lectures after doing 48-hour shifts over the weekend. Once I explained to her, I tried to make everything in the lab into a sexual reference, from zoology to botany, my wife's lab grade went from mid-B's in lab to A's. This made her extremely happy. It made it harder for me to keep beating her in the lab though.

Since college, my wife has been my best friend and partner. We have worked very hard over the years to get through medical school, then residency, our lives as attendings, and in the process of raising a family. Making it to this point is a testament to my wife's patience and persistence. We were both very intellectual. I am more the hands-on, get-the-job-done guy. My wife is a typical brainiac who can remember anything she has ever read. We make one hell of a team. We both take pride in being able to spend time with our patients. Being a successful doctor is more about taking care of people rather than the number of patients seen. A good day for me is being able to say I impacted someone's life today. Patients do not care how much you know until you show them how much you care.

Throughout my life, I have met many people who have helped steer and direct my life. It started with my parents, grandparents, other adults, and even strangers. Then it transitioned into professors and other physicians. I have even gotten direction from people like Robert Kiyosaki and Grant Cardone. The last two came later in life when I started looking at my future and financial planning. I realized I knew nothing about money or how to invest and make it compound. I realized I wanted to learn to make money work for me. I went to several conferences. I met some great people. One person in particular, Sean, has helped change my mindset and taught me how to look at business. He actually helped me start my current business/practice. He is a business-minded individual who, for some reason, saw something in me and chose to help.

I know that God has played an integral part in my life. He always seems to put the right people in place for me. As long as I stop fighting him, put my pride aside, and let him steer. I have made significant steps from where I started. It seems the people who keep crossing my path are there to challenge my current thinking. They help me if I am thinking too small. Also, my current problems seem so much smaller to people who have already done what I plan to do. It is like they have a way of letting the non-important things roll off their backs and keep moving to their next goal.

The impact on my life that the people discussed above have had are immeasurable. Starting with my grandparents from a young age, they showed me what a good traditional relationship looks like. They also helped me learn that communication is key in a relationship. My grandparents were always there for me when my parents could not be there because of work or other issues. Then my father for always being the supporter of the family. He showed me what it was like to be selfless. The individuals who were not family, as I mentioned above, seem to be strategically placed in my life at pivotal moments. I believe they were sent to help steer my life in the right direction. Sometimes their interventions required multiple meetings. However, the one meeting with a stranger at a bus stop had a big impact in my life with just a few words. These moments that I would like people to look back upon and reflect upon. Also, be open to challenges that people put in front of you to help get you to a better place in your life.

Life Lessons

1.   Never discount the words of a stranger.

2.   Who has been placed in your life to guide you?

3.   Be open to challenges from people.

Questions for the Reader

1.   When was the last time someone showed up out of the blue to help you get through a struggle?

    _____

    _____

2.   Do you believe in Divine Intervention?

    _____

    _____

3.   Do you make time to question what you want in life?

    _____

    _____

4.   What's the main takeaway from this chapter?

    _____

    _____

Chapter 13

Family Factor

What is family? Jim Butcher once said, "When everything goes to hell, the people who stand by you without flinching are your family". My family is amazing. We have been tested with difficult times. Throughout the years, we have become better people. My wife and I have worked hard to reach our point today. We are much closer now than ever before because of the fires we went through. We made agreements with each other before our wedding. These agreements have made it possible to get where we are today. We knew that we each had generational curses that had to be broken. If our future kids were going to have a chance, it was up to us to break these curses.

The first agreement was to never yell at each other. This is both at home and in public. We both had experiences in childhood where adults would argue and fight a lot while growing up. Interactions like this show everyone that you don't respect the other person. Especially if you're able to yell at someone in public. The public shame you bestow on the person you're yelling at is downright disrespectful. If you can yell at someone, you obviously believe them to be inferior to you. As for me, my wife is the person I respect the most, just under God. I can honestly say that I have not yelled at her after over 11 years of marriage. Have I wanted to? Hell yes. I've caught myself a few times. I don't want to go down that road of yelling and fighting. We can walk away for a few minutes or hours, then come back and discuss the situation. The discussions need to be held in a calm manner. Once we have calmed down, we can get to the bottom of the problem or transgression. We have both had our moments of being hotheaded over different issues throughout the years. However, communicating calmly has led us to understand each other's feelings. We can understand each other's position once things are discussed calmly. This has led us to a better relationship than most.

The second agreement was not to lie. This agreement has gotten me a lot of trouble, especially when my wife is trying something on that I don't like. I tell her that doesn't look good or a variation of something like that. She will get mad at me for a few seconds, and then life returns to normal. She prefers that I tell her the truth. Because my being able to tell her the truth, good or bad, is more important than fake compliments or so-called little white lies. Don't worry, she tells me if I am doing something dumb. Do I like it at that moment? Absolutely not, but I want a real relationship built on trust. I see too many couples today that can't critique each other. This goes for appearances in public, raising children, financial discipline, and many other things. You must be honest with yourself and your partner at all times.

The third agreement is to never go to bed angry. This one was the hardest for me, and I think for her. I grew up in a house where suppressing your feelings was the normal thing to do. If you said anything, you were whining or being ungrateful. So, you learn to bottle things up and move on with your life. Even now, sometimes my wife and I have disagreements, which require work from her and I to get the anger out in the open. If it is in the open, we can deal with it before sleeping. She will catch me still being angry and remind me of the agreement. Then we talk it out like adults. Both my wife and I have a good logical side. Being physicians, it is needed. So, we start there and understand where the other is coming from and the problem. Once the issues have been identified, dealing with them is much easier. In the end, we are typically not mad at the same things. I will be the first to admit this is not easy. Sometimes we lie there in silence until one of us can explain why we are mad. Typically, it was a miscommunication or misinterpretation of something that had been said.

It has been said that words can either sever or strengthen a relationship. Words can bring you up or tear you down. When dealing with relationships, try to be impeccable with your word. You should build your partner up. Because once you start tearing them down, it is a slippery slope. I know this from my childhood. I watched adults cut each other down with their words both behind their backs and to their faces. It is truly scary how much words can damage someone. A person's words can take over someone's life. They can become prisoners of the words that have been spoken to them.

Words can convince people that they are depressed or happy, depending on the context. I've seen patients who had been persuaded by someone they love that they were sick. These patients ended up developing symptoms of the so-called disease. They honestly thought they had the disease. In the end, they were just being played by the people they loved. Words can have that much power over someone's well-being. I strongly encourage everyone to be impeccable with their word. The more careful you are with your words, the better.

Most family issues can be fixed if you are open, honest, and treat each other with respect. That is something forgotten in today's world. This is advice for couples, all family members, or any relationship. These simple suggestions can fix a lot of relationships. Although with any relationship, you'll have to put in work. With today's divorce rate at 42%, something has to change as a society. My wife and I also had a fourth agreement. That agreement is that divorce is not an option. We will work through each scenario as it arises. However, calling it quits is not an option. These agreements were not just for us; they were for our future family. We both knew the statistics for children who grow up in broken homes on issues like incarceration, poverty, and teenage pregnancy. We knew the best way to combat the statistics for them was to stay married. The agreements were more for our children than they were for us. We knew the image we wanted to portray for our children. We also learned that the statistics for any form of child abuse go up significantly if the parents are divorced. Children who are in the home with a non-biological adult, married or otherwise, have a significantly increased risk as well. These are the reasons for the agreements. I wish my parents had these agreements before my siblings and I were born.

With the agreements that my wife and I set before our marriage, we still respect and enjoy each other's company. I am still the class clown. I was in high school, college, and medical school, and am at home. My wife will look at me and say she is never bored. My son is following in my footsteps as a goofball. He and I can wrestle on the floor for hours on end. My daughter will join us as well, and the three of us can make one heck of a ruckus in the house. My wife will sit on the couch and laugh. Occasionally, she gets caught up in chaos as well. She enjoys every moment of this. I learned the importance of family from my Grandpa and Grandma Bingham. I had to relearn this as an adult. It's funny how you forget essential things.

The time in between me leaving corporate medicine and starting my new business, I got to spend extra time with my family. I realized how much I missed doing the crazy things with them daily. I realized the joy it brings them when Dad acts goofy with them. My wife and children do much better when I'm around more. These are the people that I have worked so hard for over the years. These people right here. I'm winning as long as everyone in this house has a reasonable opinion of me. This is the family that matters above all else. Once my family at home is taken care of, I can look at my extended family. My extended family includes not only blood relatives, but also very close friends. Friends who have earned my trust and respect over the years.

Have the hard conversations with your loved ones. You are not helping anyone by staying silent. Show your love by helping someone overcome what is holding them back. This is what the best family members or friends do for the people they care about.

They will tell you when you are messing up and don't sugarcoat things. I will take one or two friends who love me enough to tell me the truth, over 1000 fake friends who talk behind my back about how I am messing up. Yes, it hurts. All growth and improvement hurts. Take your licks and improve yourself. But also, be willing to tell others how they can improve. Will it be a comfortable conversation? Nope! Will you be nervous? Yes. Is helping someone you care about more important than your comfort? Absolutely, it is. So be that one friend who always tells the truth to your friends.

My wife and I are planning for our family's future after we are gone. I am shaping my family's future to how we want it. We are not listening to the standard narrative (Join a corporation and work there for 20+ years). We are going to make our own path to financial freedom. We are only going to invest in things that make sense to us. I will only invest in things that create cash flow and appreciate over time. Some investment cash flow will improve, and others' appreciation will improve. I myself prefer tangible assets, businesses, and real estate. My wife likes to play with stocks and futures. We are playing the game of investing to secure our future.

No one ever got rich by working a 9-to-5 job for someone else. Investing or creating is the only way to get rich and find financial freedom. There are no shortcuts. You have to change your mindset to get to this point. I taught a little about economic freedom in this book; however, there will be future books on the subject. Just know, we have reached a point where we can invest and secure our freedom. We are now at a point in our lives where we are investing in our own business, real estate, and the stock market. We're going to create generational wealth for our family.

If you listen to normal people, you will be normal. Why be normal when you can be extraordinary? You wouldn't be reading this book if you were normal. You're reading it to hopefully gain insights and lessons from my life. This sets you apart from the rest of the crowd. Everyone has things in their own lives that set them apart from everyone else. I highly suggest you listen to it.

As I stated previously, if you want to be "normal", you'll work at a corporate job for 20+ years, have a mediocre marriage, and hopefully be able to pass down some small inheritance to your children and grandchildren. However, this is too boring for me. Life is a game; some days you win and others you lose. Take chances! Be willing to take the success chance. This is what sets millionaires and billionaires apart from "normal people". Millionaires and billionaires are eager to take chances. Sometimes you must have the courage and drive to do what others would not do. In life, there are no guarantees; every investment comes with risk. I can't promise your investments will succeed. But consider the risk of never investing in yourself or something else; you miss 100% of the shots you don't take.

That corporate job that you have could be gone tomorrow. Big corporations today treat you as numbers, not as people. Why do you owe them any sense of loyalty? I used to believe in company loyalty. This changed for me in my 30s. There's no need for loyalty to organizations that treat you like numbers. Your loyalty is to God, your family, and your responsibility to be successful. For me, being successful has evolved over the years. As a child, being successful for me was becoming a Navy SEAL. As a teenager, after being diagnosed with type 1 diabetes, success just meant not dying that day. In my 20s, being successful was graduating from college and then medical school. In my 30s, it has changed to enjoying my time with friends, family, and creating generational wealth for the rest of my family. It is my duty and responsibility.

My wife and I are investing in our children's financial future, education, and protection. With the focus on our children's future and brain development, we have decided to take our children out of public schools. We have decided to homeschool. She was homeschooled, so she liked the idea but struggled to balance working a corporate job and being home with the kids. Creating our own business solved that conundrum for her. Another benefit to homeschooling is that I can teach the children real-life examples. We can show the children how to run a business. We can show the children how to buy properties. We can teach them how to cook, care for a house, fix or build things, do their taxes, or speak properly and confidently. These are not taught in modern schools.

The modern-day school system kills creativity. The school system today was formed for the Industrial Revolution. This system was to prepare a compliant workforce. They do this in today's school system by using standardized curriculum, age-segregation, age-based progression, a rigid timetable with bells telling children when to complete each task, and lesson plans geared towards standardized testing. The school system kills creativity, focuses on compliance, emphasizes only one correct answer, prioritizes only working alone, and discourages student collaboration. Corporations want workers who do not challenge the status quo; schools prepare students for that. They (the government and corporations) would prefer a less intelligent society they can control more easily. This is why the USA is consistently at the bottom for education worldwide.

One of the other benefits of homeschooling is teaching my children how to become responsible adults. By keeping them home, you are not relying on the school system to teach your children how to be responsible adults. Hell, in today's school system, they can't even tell boys from girls. No, thank you!! There are teachers within the public-school systems who are using their platform and position of authority to poison children's minds to fit the teacher's world/political views. These teachers prey on children when their minds are developing and confuse them greatly. This was unheard of when I was a child. I'll take the responsibility of teaching them and developing their worldview myself. If you see your school system doing these things, please teach your children at home or send them to a private school.

I get to teach my son how a man is supposed to treat a woman and how to act in society. Not this new watered-down version of manliness that's being shoved down everyone's throats with this anti-masculinity nonsense. I get to teach my daughter how she is supposed to be treated. She will know what a good man is. My children will know what is expected in a good partner as well. They should find partners and work with them to achieve their goals together. My children will be my most significant achievement in this world. My goal is to make them better than I ever could be. Then I will leave things in my children's capable hands.

My being dyslexic was tough to catch when I was growing up. It was tough because of where I lived and the resources available. It wasn't until I was in college that I could explain what was going on when I was trying to read, and with the help of friends and professors, I caught up. Nowadays, there is better awareness of people with dyslexia than there was when I was growing up. I don't blame any of the teachers for not catching it or my parents. It's just another challenge that needs to be overcome. The majority of the teachers at Bray-Doyle, Oklahoma, were like second parents. They cared about their students. It wasn't just me that they cared about. They had a connection with all the kids in their classes. Heck, even our high school principal, whom I got to see a couple of times when I was in trouble, was a great father figure. We knew what was expected of us. Yes, I receive swats a couple of times. They were all justified. Boys, being boys, will get into trouble. I look back at the scenarios and I just laugh. I do feel a little bit bad sometimes about the things we did to our AG teacher, like welding all the welding machines in a grain feeder, but it was all in good fun. He was a very patient man. He would just shake his head and laugh at us. He did spend a lot of time with my friends and me since we were in FFA as well as his AG class.

Family has always been an interesting concept for me. Yes, I believe that family is the people who stick with you whenever you're going through rough times. Family is more than just blood. I have gained family members who are not blood-related throughout my life. Some of these family members include co-residents from residency or colleagues from work. Durin and Disa, the co-chiefs I mentioned in the residency chapter, have remained close to us and our children for many years. Even though we live several states away, they remain essential to our lives. Even though they're not in our everyday world, I can call them with issues or concerns. That road goes both ways. They can contact us with anything as well. Anytime we go back to Oklahoma. We try to hang out with them.

Yes, extended family is important and has an important place. My advice for a young couple about to be married or any reader is to realize that once someone is married, they form their own new nuclear family. That is the family that they will spend their time and energy with. Everyone else is extended family. I know everyone means well when they want to include everyone at every event. A young couple can't be at every event, especially if the parents are separated. It creates stress for the young couple that doesn't need to be there. The young couple is making their own traditions for their new family. Because the husband or wife and children, as they come, are the primary family now, it took me a long time to realize this. Now, at extended family gatherings, I don't have a problem saying no, we can't make it. I do not feel bad anymore. This has made it so that we enjoy holidays much more. We can relax and be ourselves.

In this chapter, I want you to figure out who your family is. Your family does not have to be blood-related. Your family is the people who have supported you and helped you succeed during hard times. I cannot find where the saying originated, but it hits deep. "Never go to dinner with people who wouldn't go to battle with you". I understand that sounds extreme, but it has a great point. If you waste time and energy on people who don't matter, you take away from those who do.

Life Lessons

1. Learn to discern your immediate family from your extended family.

2. Keep your inner circle very small.

3. Set up agreements with yourself and your spouse.

Questions for the Reader

1. Who is in your immediate family?

   _____

   _____

2. Who would battle with you?

   _____

   _____

3. What's the main takeaway from this chapter?

   _____

   _____

Conclusion

It has been one heck of a ride. If you had told me when I was an eight-year-old in Bray, Oklahoma, I would be a physician who has lived in multiple states, own real estate, and have a business. I would have told you that you were freaking nuts!! My life has changed numerous times over the years. I have had some hard times. I have had some good times. I've also had several instances of amazing times. I had to endure hard times to get to the good stuff.

This story started as a collection of stories and reflections for myself, a way to help me pin down and work through some of the hidden anger issues I had as an adult. My goal was never to write a book. My goal was to help myself find peace with what was troubling me. As an adult, I had a lot of deep-seated anger issues. I did not want to pass them on to my children. Therefore, I put in the work with a professional coach. It was my coach who suggested writing down the struggles of my life. It doesn't matter how small or big they seem; write them down. It was his way of helping me with the catharsis of my soul. After a few sessions of writing my challenges down and talking them through with my coach, Daniel Gomez, he suggested I go even further in my writing. He asked me to write about what I did to overcome the challenges or what good came from the situations. After a few months of doing this, I asked

I asked my wife to look at the document on the computer. She then advised me that I had a good story and should share it. She did suggest that she proofread everything, though. I write the way I talk. This was not the first time I've heard I should write a book. Daniel Gomez, my coach, said that I needed to publish a book and share Dr. Charles Bingham's story with the world.

However, I wasn't sure I wanted my story out there. I had typical fears: what if I offend someone with my story, or what if people disown me? Then I decided I typically don't care what people think. Why should I know? As the stories developed, and I was sure I would be talking about things that happened in my childhood, I felt it might upset some family members. I realized that this is my story. If they were perceived as villains in my story, that is how I felt about it then, and ultimately grew because of it. The people who truly matter will be there with me in the end. So, ultimately, I decided my story was worth writing down, and my concerns weren't a justification to prevent me from writing it and hopefully helping someone.

Then I realized how much writing the story improved my outlook. I went from being angry all the time to being a calmer individual. I do not have the feeling of dread weighing me down daily anymore. If this story helps one person, then it was a success. For the record, it has already done that. It has helped me be a better father, husband, son, brother, and friend.

The challenges in my life are not unique. People deal with adversity every day. What makes me unique is that I did not let the adversities restrict my growth or potential. My challenge for everyone reading this book is to develop a mindset like mine. Adopt an "I will not be broken" or, as David Goggins says, "you can't hurt me" outlook. Life is mean. Life is a cruel beast if you let it be. Life will beat you up. It will leave you battered and bruised. It is up to you to keep getting back up, take a stand, and push forward.

My family has been the most significant source of inspiration for me. My family started inspiring me from a very young age. My grandparents showed me how they worked through their issues and communicated. They also stood for what was right, even though it led to difficult times and conversations. Then my father showed me how to work hard to provide and ensure we had what we needed. He sacrificed his peace of mind to keep us safe and fed. Then my wife and children inspire me to be a better person every day. They are the ones who inspired me to become healthy. They're the ones that inspired me to look into investing for our futures. My wife and children will continue to be a source of inspiration for me to push further than I've ever pushed before.

My extended family has also inspired me, especially more recently. When I say immediate family, I refer to my wife and children; they are the most important people in my world. My extended family has also overcome obstacles and is becoming much better people. I am happy to report that both my mother and sister are currently working through their addictions and overcoming their inner demons.

My mother has been clean from opioids and benzodiazepines for two years. She is now able to come around my family more. She tells me all the time that my putting up boundaries and blocking her from my wife and children's lives caused her to take a deep look at herself. She came to the realization that she was an addict. She also realized that something needed to change or she was going to be another statistic of prescription drug overdose. She didn't know how hooked she was until she took my sister to an AA meeting. Since that time, she has started working in AA to become who she should be. She has gone through the steps and started seeing how her life choices affected her children and our father. She is now leading some of the AA meetings and telling her story to help other people who are addicts. I am delighted that she is working through her issues.

My sister is working to improve herself as well. We have only recently begun to communicate again. I believe we are on a better path now than we've been in the past 2 decades. I think that she will someday understand why I had to leave. She occasionally still looks at me as the villain in her life, but she seems to see the truth now. The truth is, I never stopped caring for her, and I never stopped loving her. Yes, she is an addict, but she was always my little sister. Looking back, I'm not sure I would've done anything different. I am just glad she is starting to move forward in a good direction in her life now. She is working a good job, building up her confidence. She is starting to see that she is good at it. She is worthy of love and respect. She can achieve goals that she sets for herself. I am glad that she is now at a place where we can have a relationship, even if it is a long-distance relationship.

My brother is a great family man. He always puts his family first now. He has worked through a lot of his issues and internalized dysfunction from our parents about what marriage should look like. He is happy with his life. He and his wife are happier than they have ever been. They can communicate better now than at the beginning of their marriage. He is the classic older brother who will always give me hell, but he is also the brother who will go to bat for me if needed. I never had to deal with bullies in school because I had an older brother. He and my dad will forever be some of my biggest supporters.

My father is much more at peace and present now. He always loved his children unconditionally. However, he avoided being home a lot as we grew up. I do understand the challenges he had with coming home to deal with mom; she would drive anyone crazy back then. My father and mother divorced shortly after I got into medical school. He is remarried now. He and his new wife are doing very well. He finally has someone who puts his needs first. I am glad he is getting that type of love. I enjoy watching the man he has become as a papa. He is in his mid-60s but still gets on the floor and even wrestles with the grandchildren. I do have to tell them not to hurt him though. My dad will do everything he can to be at all the special events for his children and grandchildren. He doesn't mind traveling across the country for birthdays or graduations. He is what a parent and grandparent should be. He understands the importance of family.

These, plus many more people, are the ones who shaped me into who I am today. Currently, I have my own medical practice called Ascent Healthcare in Tennessee. The challenges with corporate medicine led me to the point of opening my own clinic. I believe I can do medicine better than most organizations. I will say, each Organization has its strengths. However, I think the future of healthcare in America needs to return to physicians who practice independently from an organization. This will disrupt the monopoly that big organizations have on the healthcare field over time. It will take some time for this to occur. But in the end, we need to get back to physicians and patients dictating what is right for the individual patient. Not some health care administration, pharmaceutical company, or insurance company makes decisions on patients they have never met. This is why my practice is patient-centered. Patients get treated for what they need. Most musculoskeletal issues can be fixed with a knowledgeable physician and a patient willing to do the work. As an Osteopathic Physician, this is part of my core tenets.

1. The Body is a Unit: The body, mind, and spirit are interconnected and function as a whole.

2. The Body is Capable of Self-Regulation, Self-Healing, and Health Maintenance: The body has an inherent ability to heal itself and maintain health.

3. Structure and Function are Reciprocally Interrelated: The body's structure (bones, muscles, organs) affects how it functions, and vice versa.

4. Rational Treatment is Based Upon an Understanding of the Basic Principles of Body Unity, Self-Regulation, and the Interrelationship of Structure and Function: Osteopathic treatment aims to restore the body's natural ability to heal by addressing structural imbalances and supporting the body's self-healing mechanisms.

As for me, I continue to grow daily as a person. I continue to use the same principles that got me here to where I am today. I keep moving forward, no matter what is thrown at me. I trust myself now more than I ever have. My strengths are well known to me now. I have a support system crucial to my success, and I know that now. I would not be here without the help of friends, family, and even strangers. These blessings have come into my life and helped me through even my darkest times.

I found a trick that helped me through the roughest times in life. I will teach it to you. If you are stuck in a situation you don't want to be in, look in the mirror. Once you look in the mirror, realize it is you who will keep you where you are or get you out of your adversity. Trust me. I know this is one of the hardest pills to swallow. It was for me. It will be painful, especially in today's world, where everyone looks to blame everyone and everything for their troubles. Taking ownership of your own inadequacies is a unique concept. It is up to you to figure out workarounds for these inadequacies. I know it is a hard way of looking at yourself. But once you understand yourself, your strengths, and your inadequacies, you can plan better. You can't ask for help until you've discovered where the issues lie. I have people who help with the things I can't or don't want to do. No one person can do all things.

As I sit here trying to think about the best way to conclude this book, I reflect on the highlights about pushing forward even when you're not sure of the next step; having faith in God and in yourself, being able to find the lightness in the dark; and being willing to listen to other people with more experience than you. More than anything, it's about hope. Hope in yourself. Hope in what you can accomplish. And hope in what God can do through you. You will be challenged in life. That you can expect. I hope to have shown you that it doesn't matter where you come from, what you've been through, or where you are currently. How you overcome these obstacles defines your life and your growth in your journey. It's hope and determination that will get you over the hurdle.

Do you run and hide or face the obstacle head-on and beat it? Just like in my high-school football career, I prefer to face the challenges head-on. I try to knock things down and bull rush through. This technique has worked for me many times. I use this approach because it fits my personality—I'm very direct. I have realized that staying true to yourself and occasionally having fun will get you through a lot.

Anyone reading this book should ask themselves, "Are you willing to face life's adversities? Are you willing to keep moving forward when it hurts or when people tell you it is impossible? The answers to these questions will determine your future. Please answer those questions honestly. You need to write them on paper. It is up to you, and it always has been.

Life Lessons
1.   Know who you are!!
2.   Know what you want in Life and why.
3.   Get people who have similar goals to help push you.

Questions for the Reader

1.   Do you schedule time to remember who you are in life?

_____

_____

2.   Do you make time to question what you want in life?

_____

_____

3.   What's a main takeaway from this chapter?

_____

_____

www.ingramcontent.com/pod-product-compliance
Lightning Source LLC
Chambersburg PA
CBHW051621120626
46551CB00014B/1899